Waterford Ontario and Area in Photos, Saving Our History One Photo at a Time

Photography
by Barbara Raué
2012

Series Name:
Cruising Ontario

Book 12: Waterford

Cover photo: Waterford Baptist Church, 68 Main Street South

Series Name: Cruising Ontario

Book 1: London
Book 2: Dundas
Book 3: Hamilton
Book 4: Oakville
Book 5: Chesley
Book 6: Stoney Creek
Book 7: Waterdown
Book 8: Owen Sound
Book 9: Mount Forest
Book 10: Dundalk
Book 11: Burford and Area
Book 12: Waterford and Area

Other Books by Barbara Raue

Coins and Gems

Arrows, Indians and Love

The Life and Times of Barbara
Volume 1: Inventions That Have Enhanced My Life
Volume 2: Entertainment That I Have Enjoyed
Volume 3: East Coast Trip 2009
Volume 4: Olympics
Volume 5: Wonders of the World

Waterford

Waterford is located on Pleasant Ridge Road, or old Highway 24 in Norfolk County, south of Brantford, north of Simcoe and southwest of Ohsweken. Waterford was established in 1794 with saw and grist mills on Nanticoke Creek. An early major industry was the agricultural implement factory built by James Green, a local merchant. The area surrounding the town is primarily agricultural land with tomatoes, tobacco and corn among the main crops. With the decline of the tobacco industry, area farmers have suffered, but ginseng is being grown on some farms. In 1979 a freak tornado swept through the town, knocked down trees, and damaged houses and public property.

Ohsweken

Ohsweken is a village on the Six Nations of the Grand River First Nation Indian Reserve. It is located on Chiefswood Road and 4th Line, southeast of Brantford. The six nations are Mohawk, Oneida, Onondaga, Cayuga, Seneca and Tuscarora.

Hartford

Hartford is located on Norfolk Country Road 74 and Highway 19 just south of the Indian Reserve.

Bealton

Bealton is located on Villa Nova Road and Highway 19.

Boston

Boston is located on Highway 4,Cockshutt Road and Highway 19.

Oakland

Oakland is located on Highway 24 and Regional Road 4, northeast of Waterford and southwest of Brantford.

*****

Ohsweken Homes and Buildings

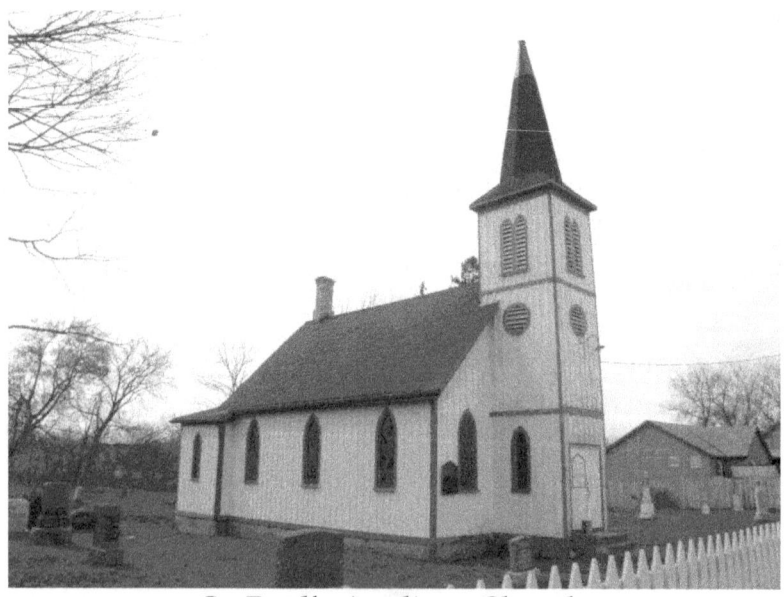

St. Paul's Anglican Church

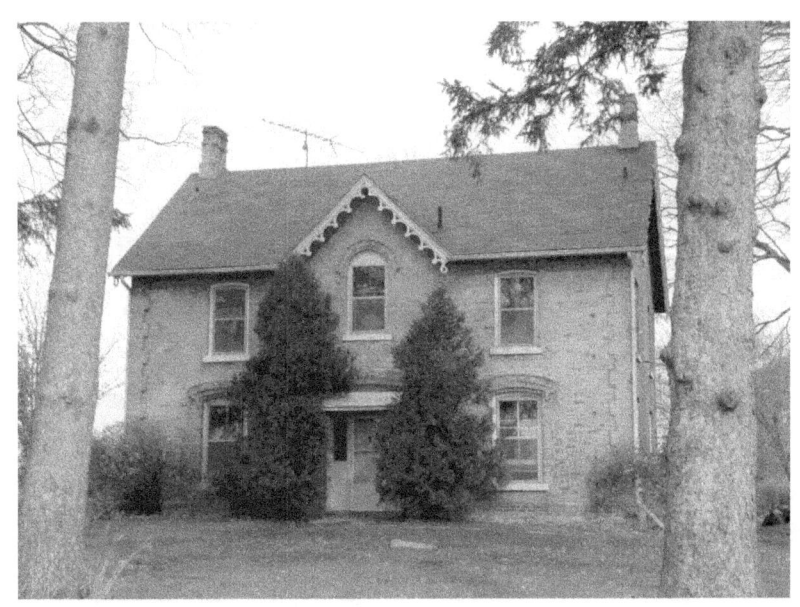

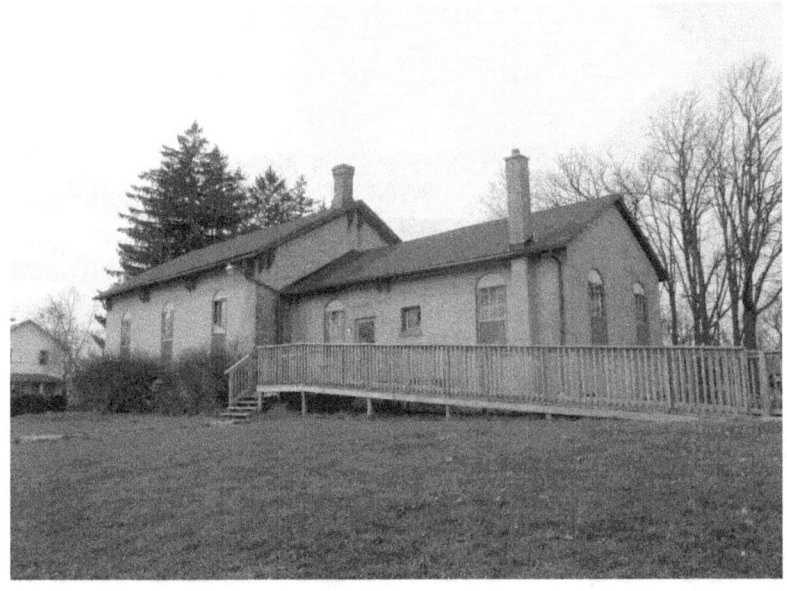

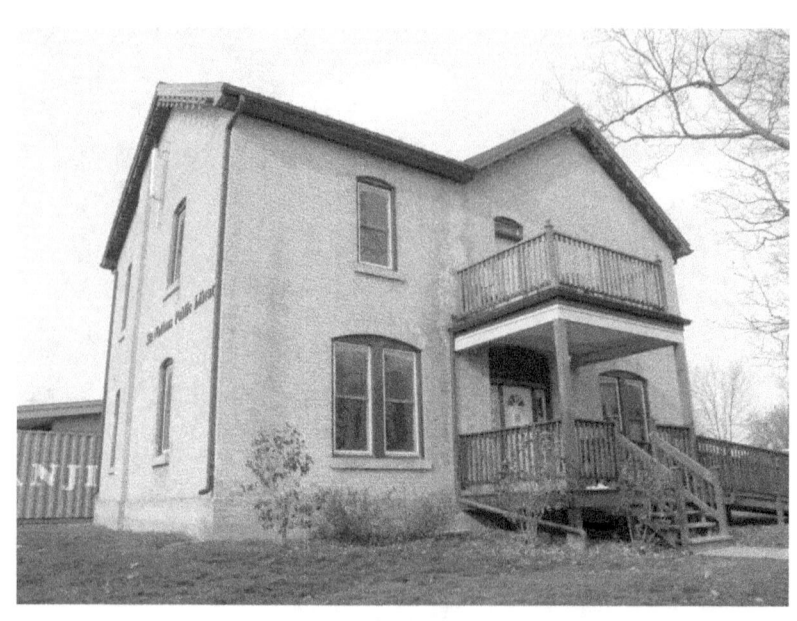

Six Nations Public Library

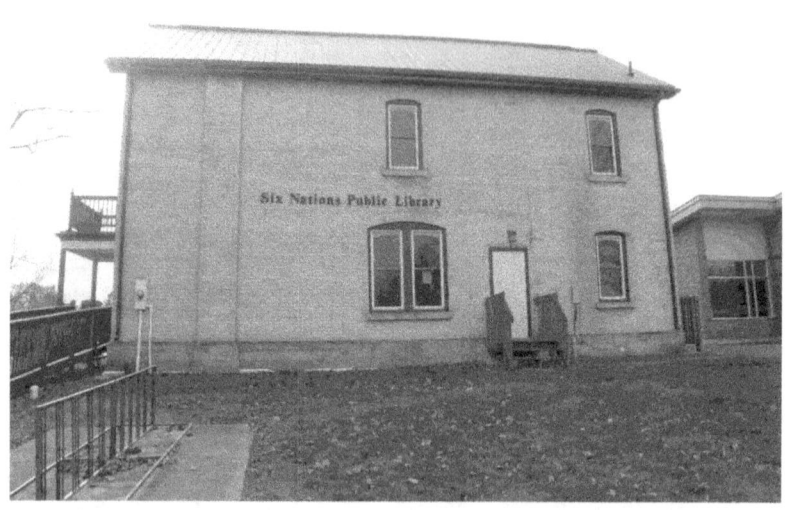

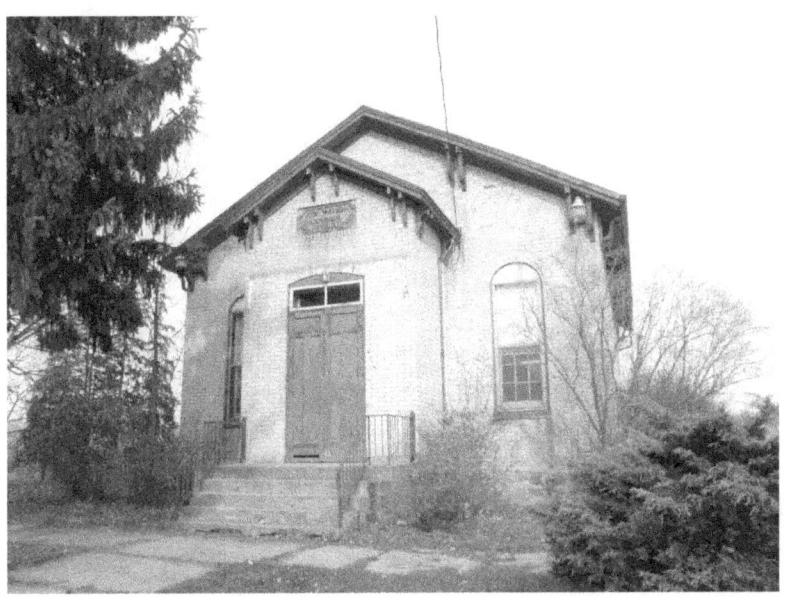

Six Nation Council 1863

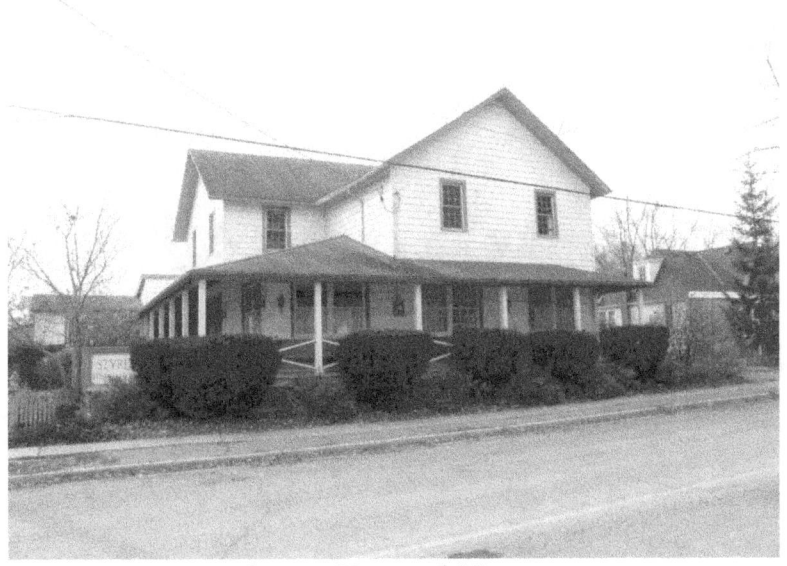

Styres Funeral Home

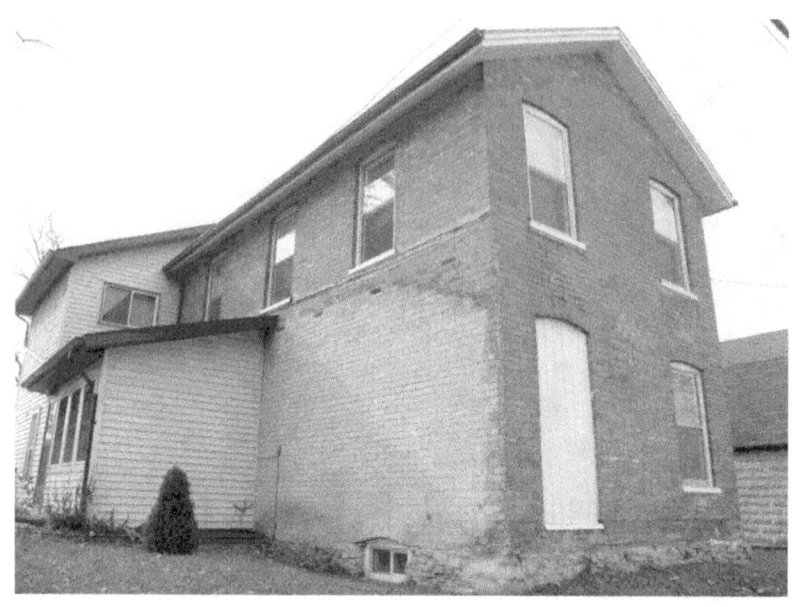

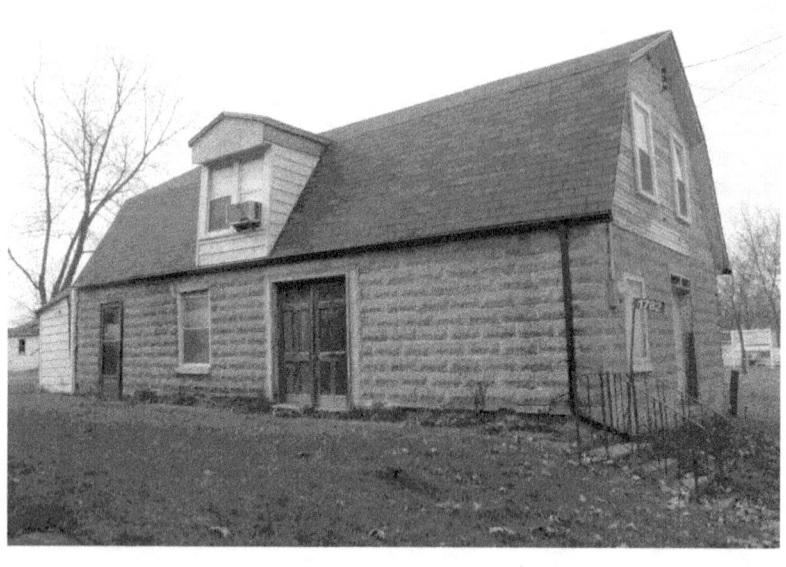

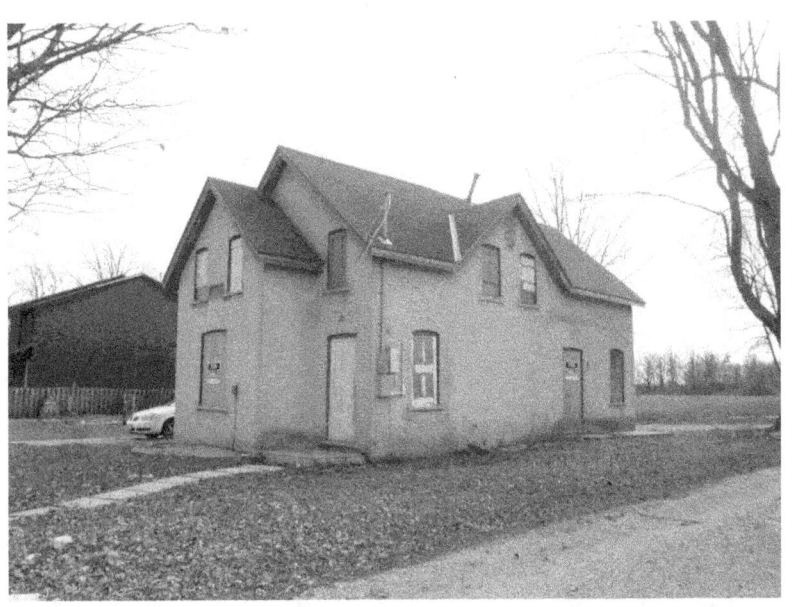

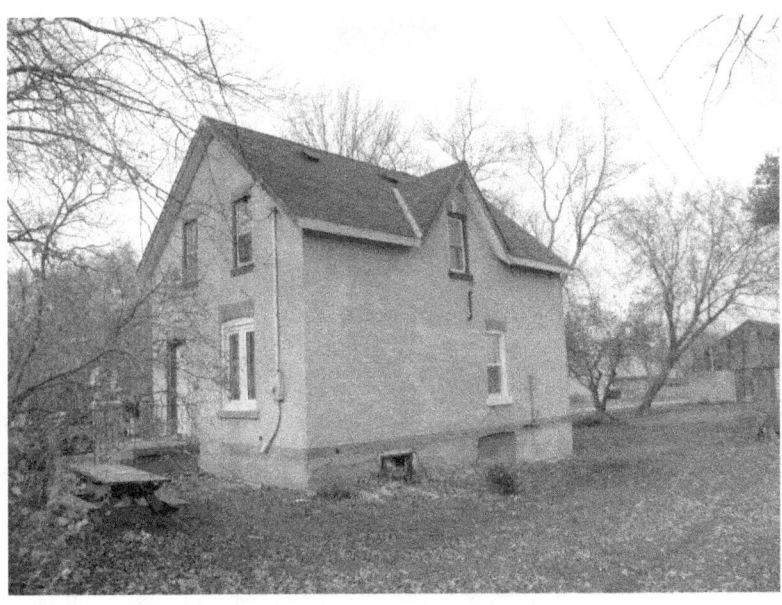

Hartford

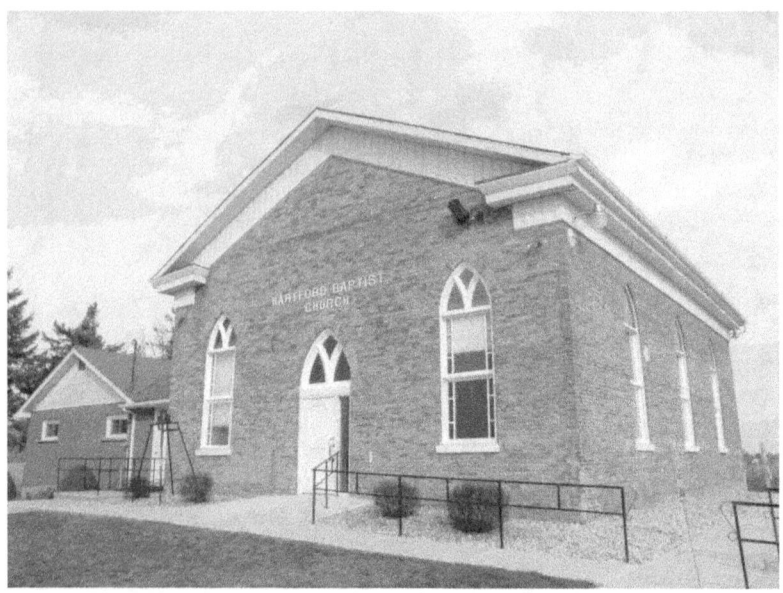

Hartford Baptist Church – established 1834
2700 County Line 74

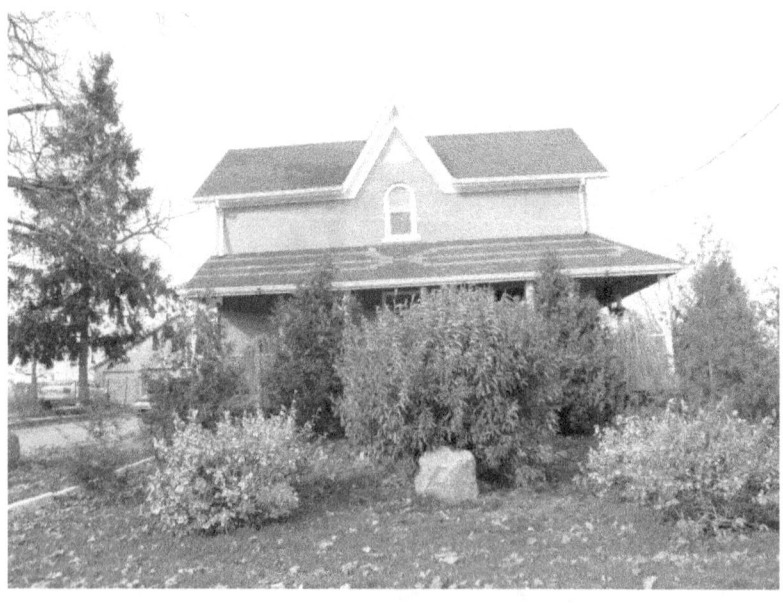

Bealton

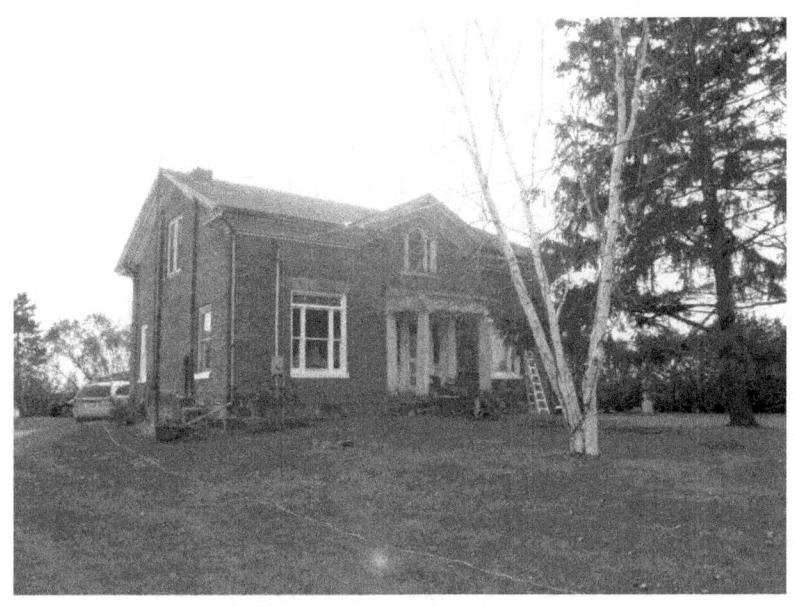

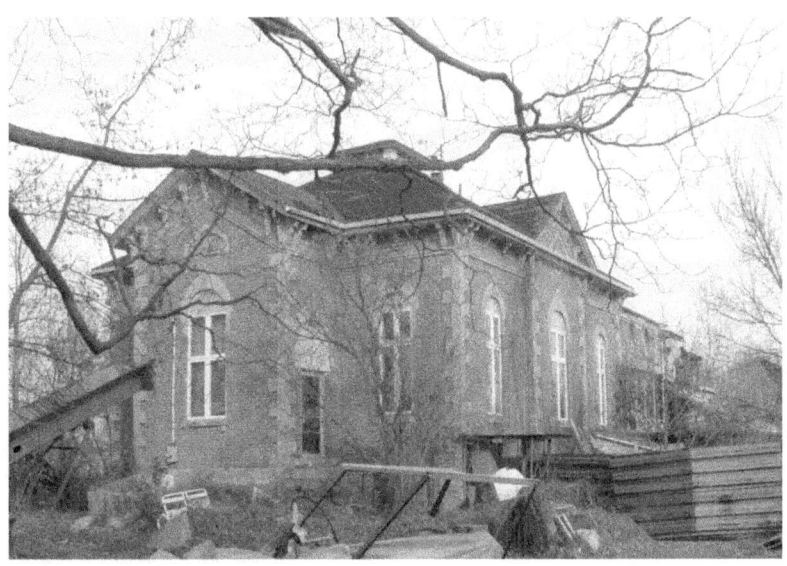

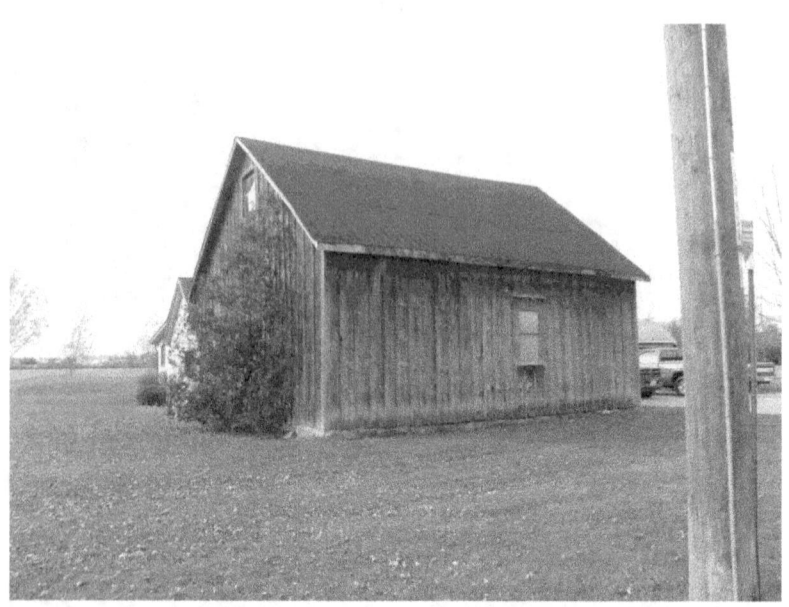

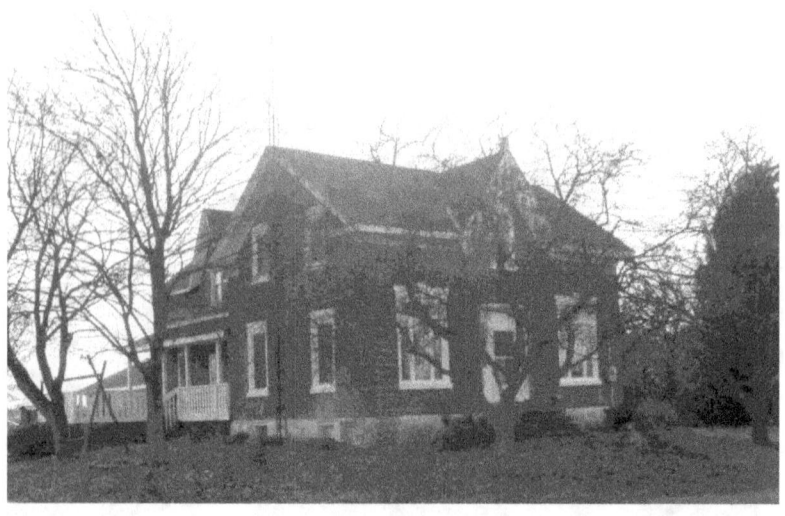

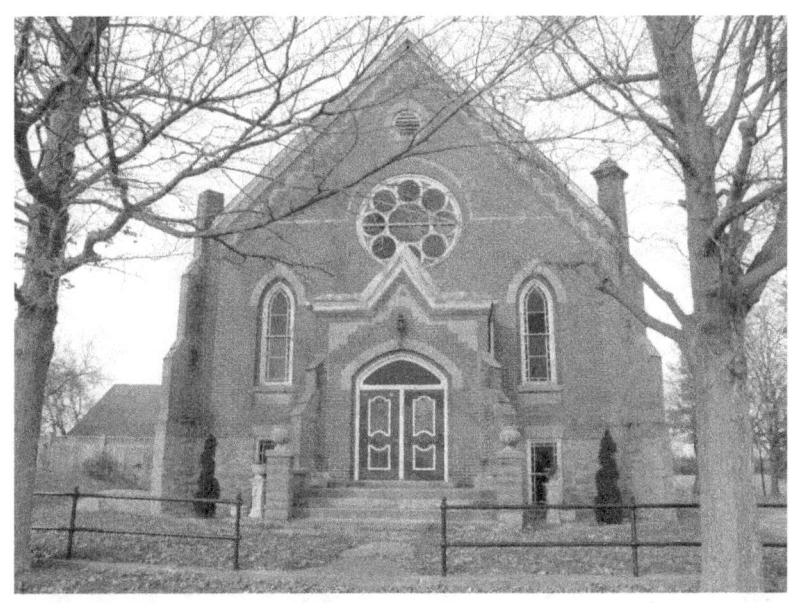

Methodist Church 1890

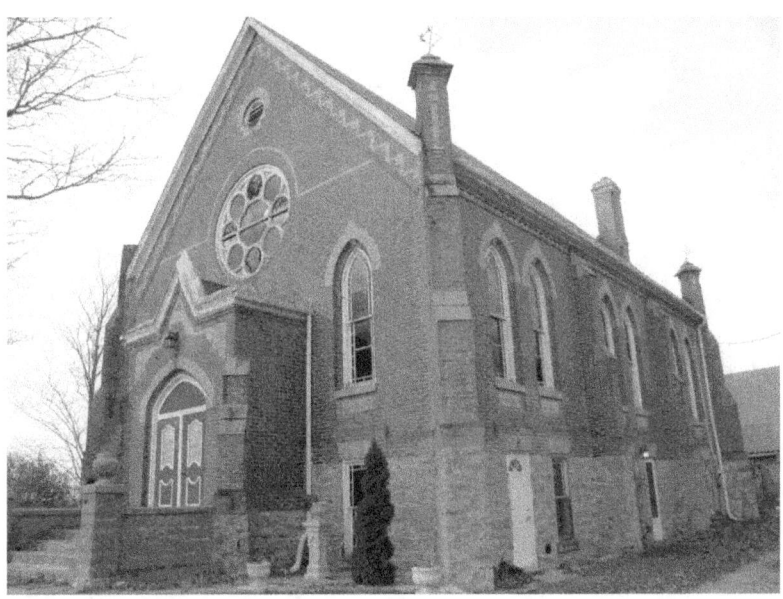

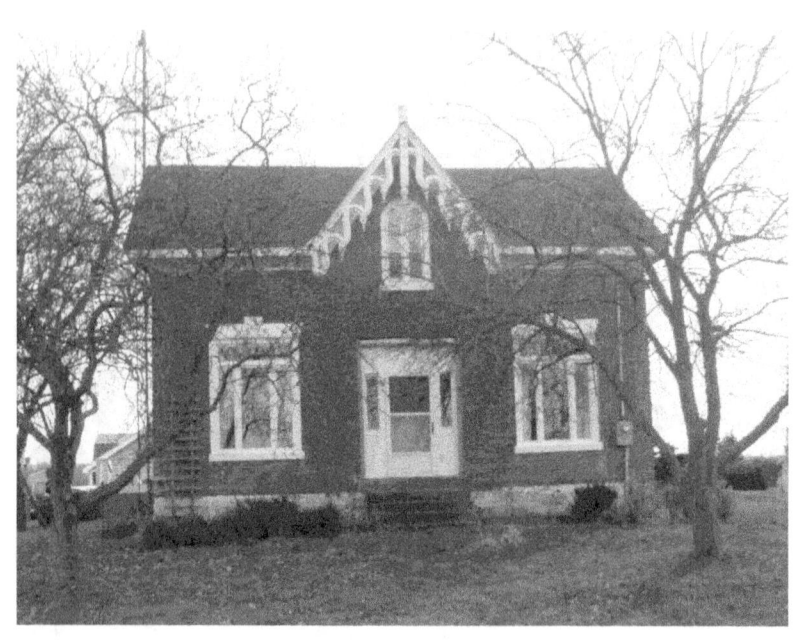

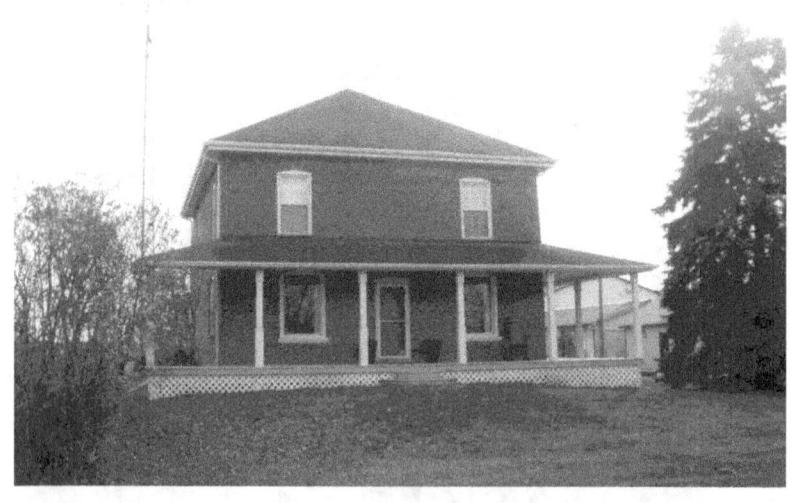

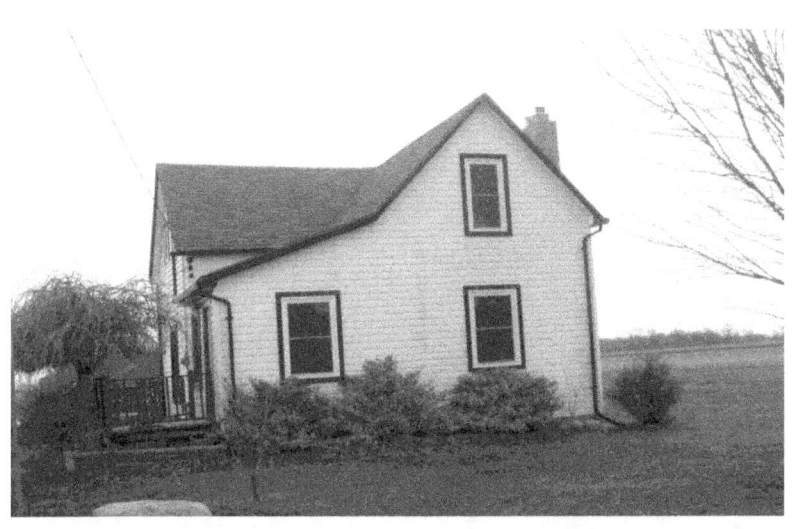

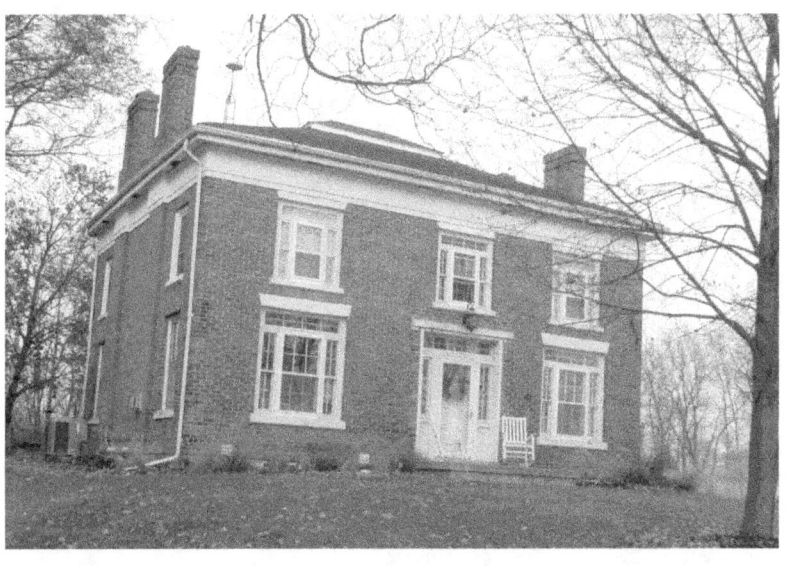

Boston

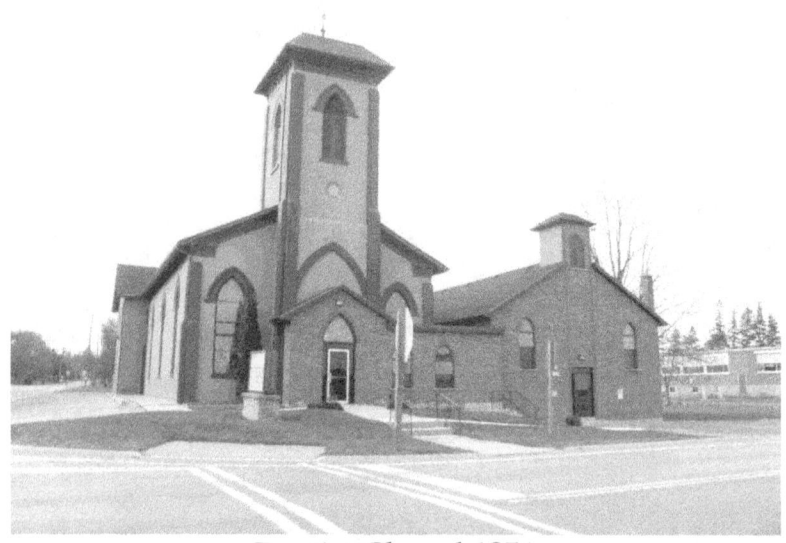

Baptist Chapel 1851

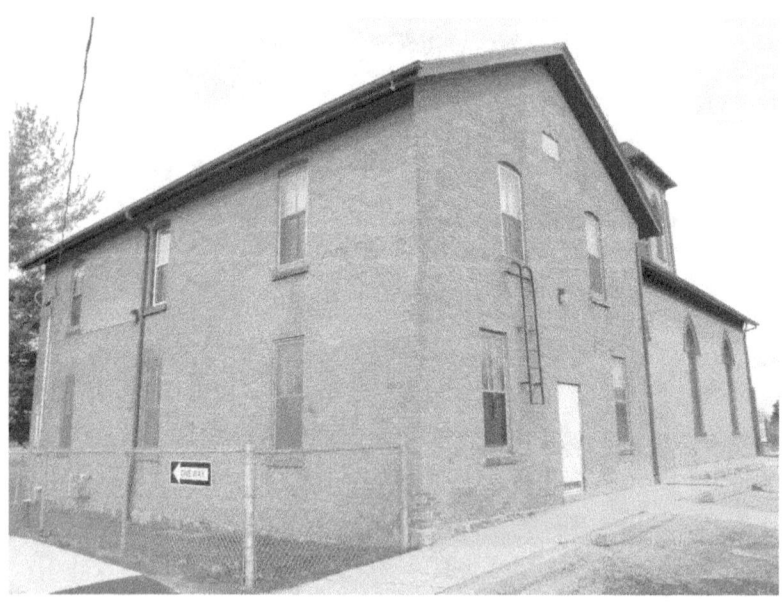

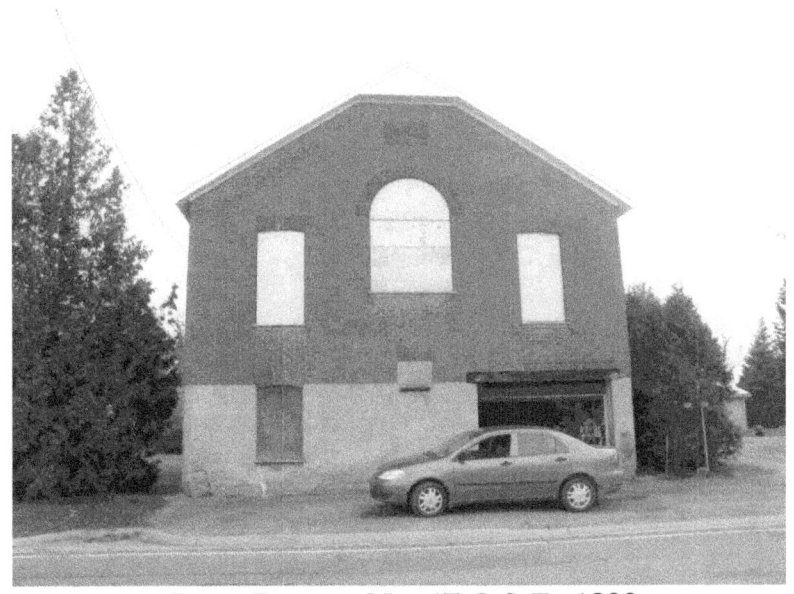

Court Boston, No. 47 C.O.F., 1899

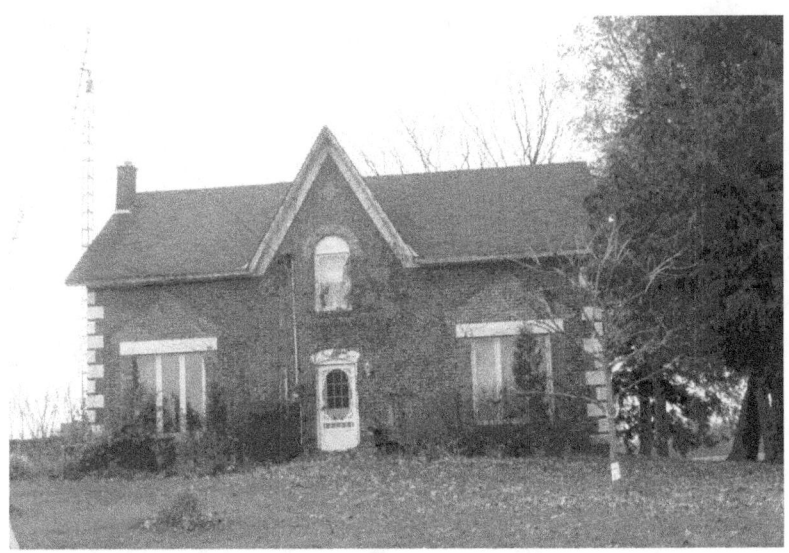

Waterford

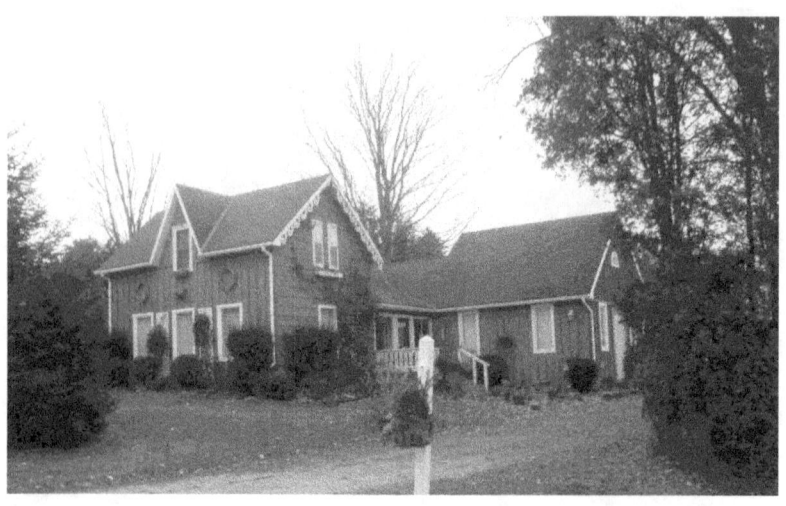

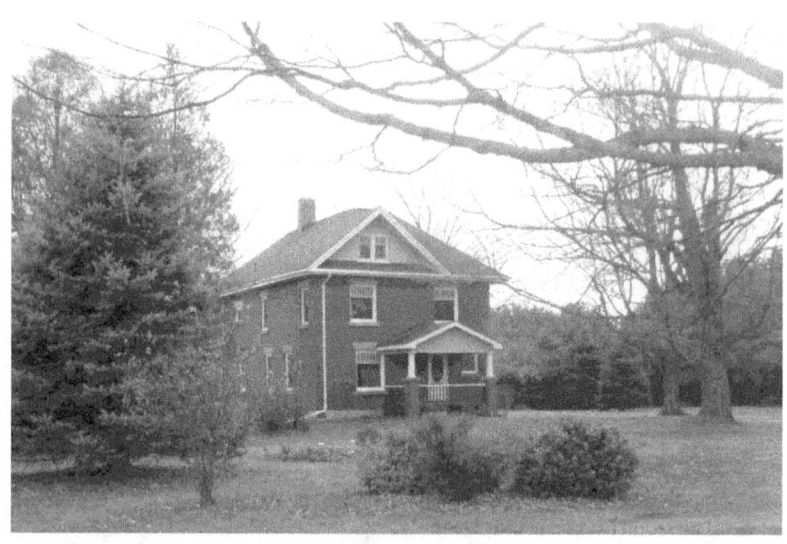

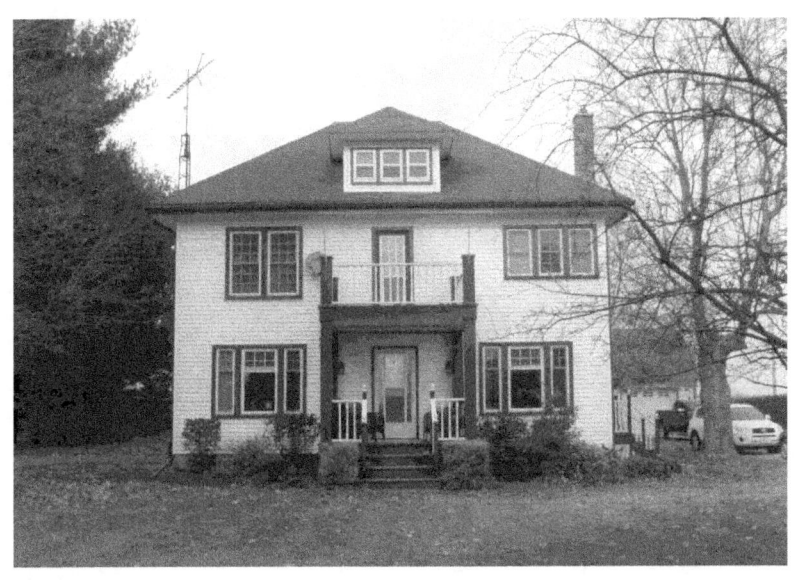

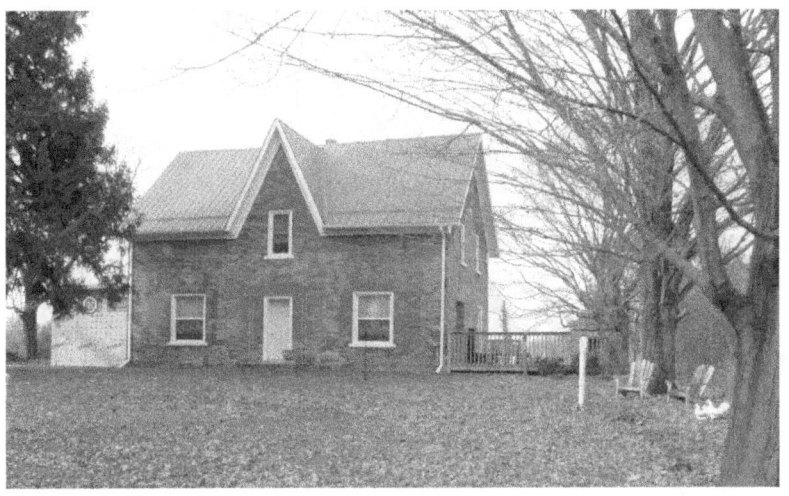

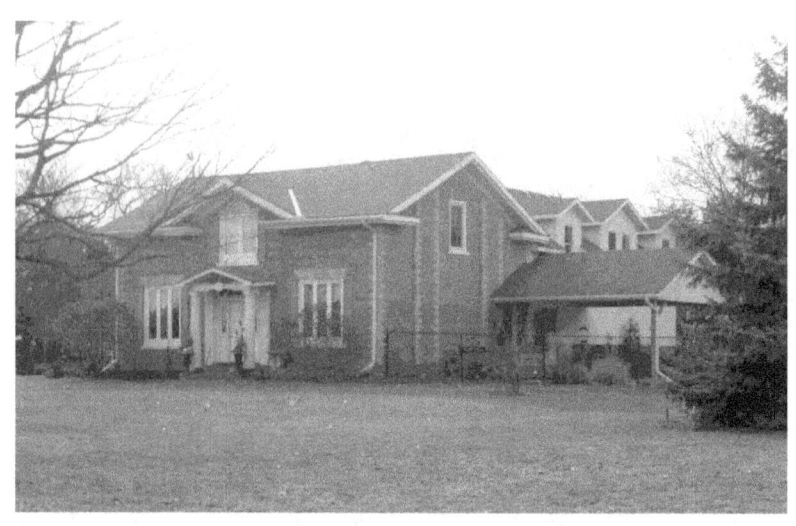

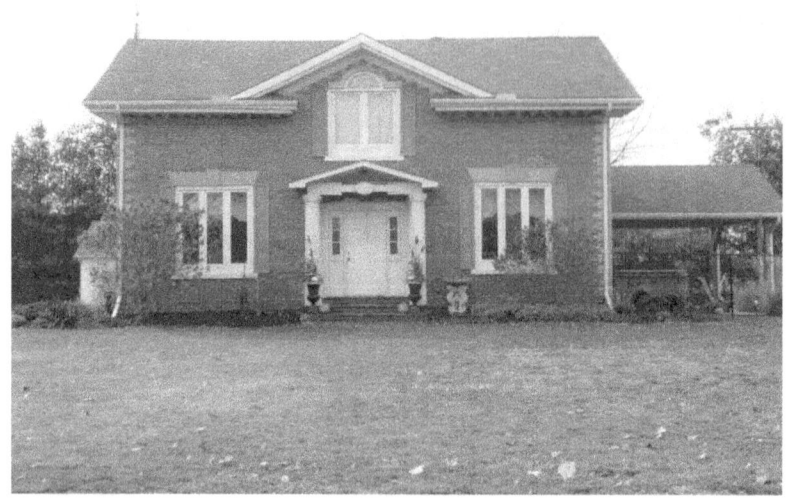

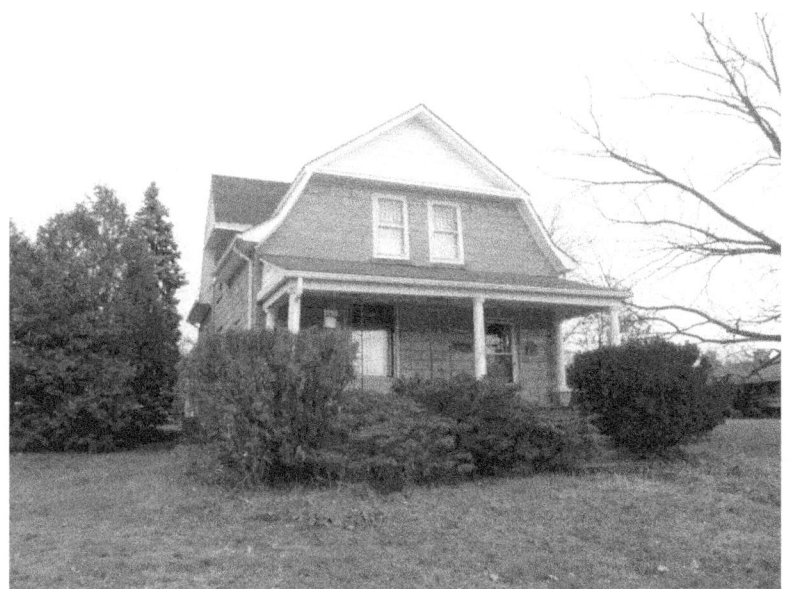

#241

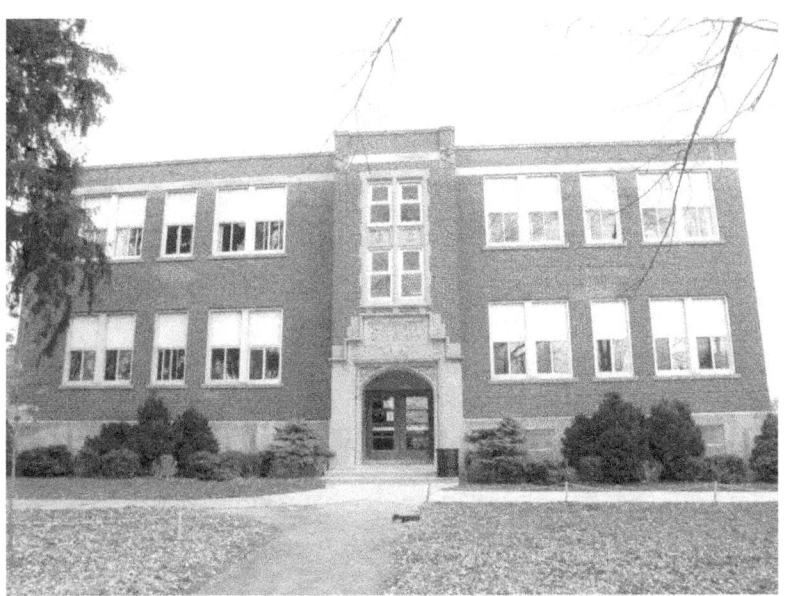

Waterford High School
227 Main Street
1892, 1931, 1936

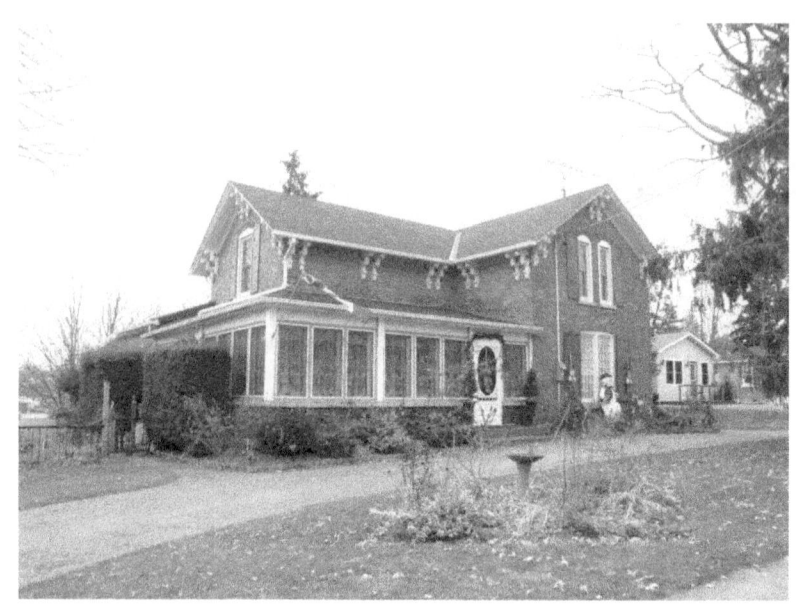

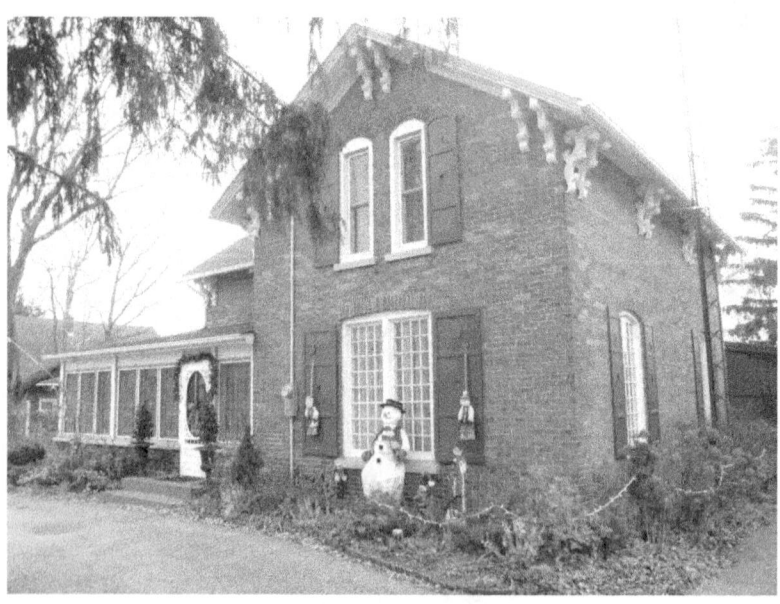

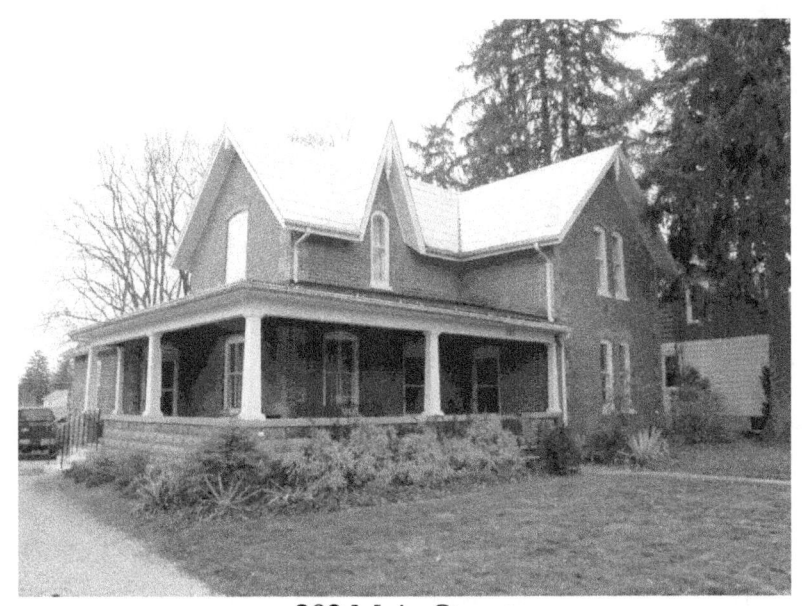

202 Main Street

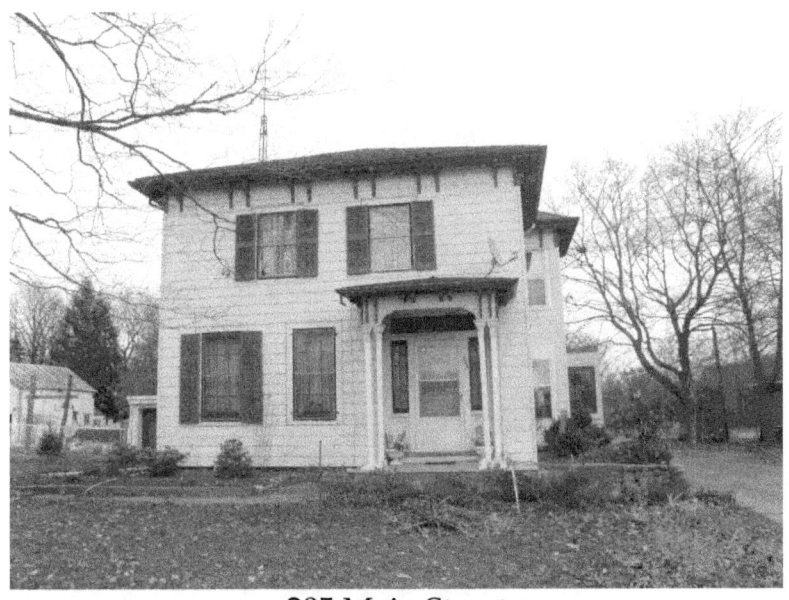

205 Main Street

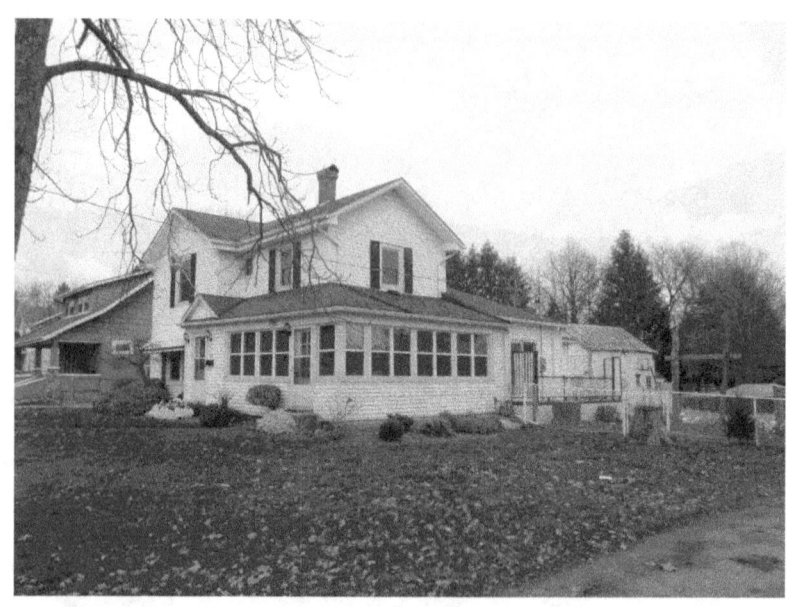

199 Main Street

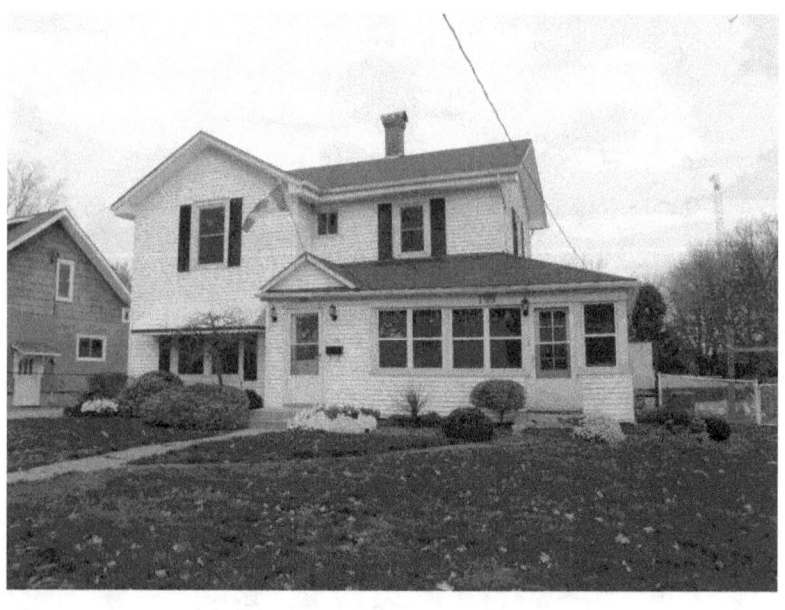

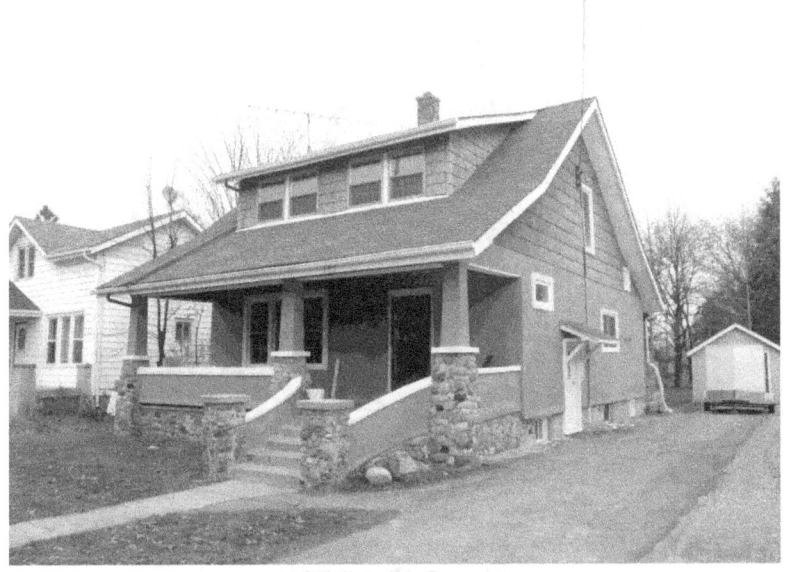

195 Main Street

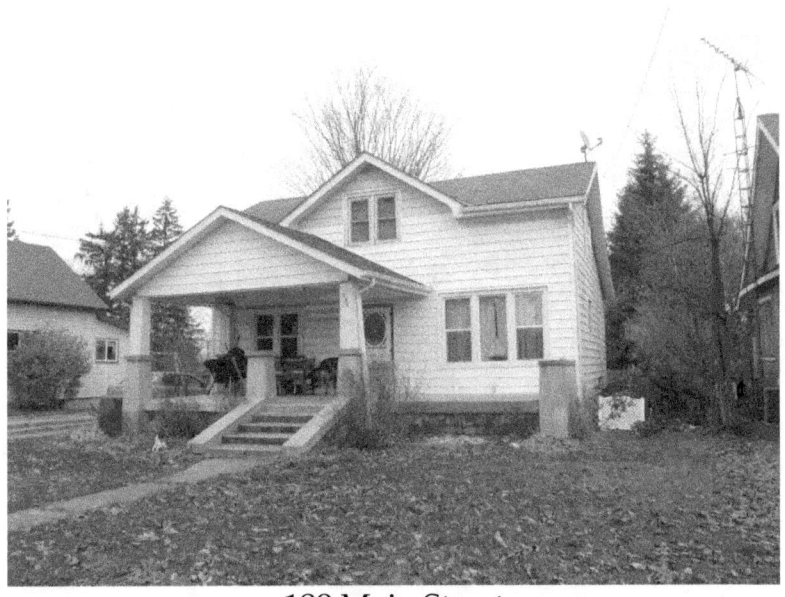

189 Main Street

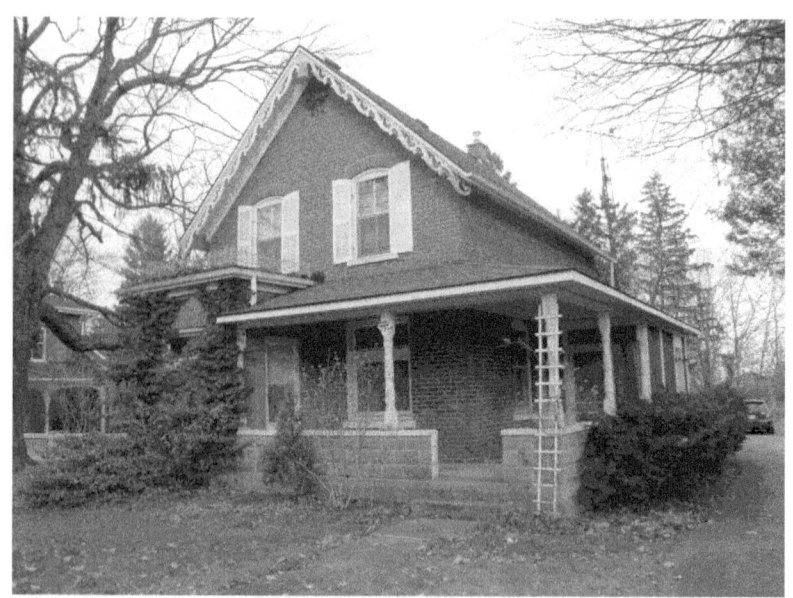

181 Main Street South

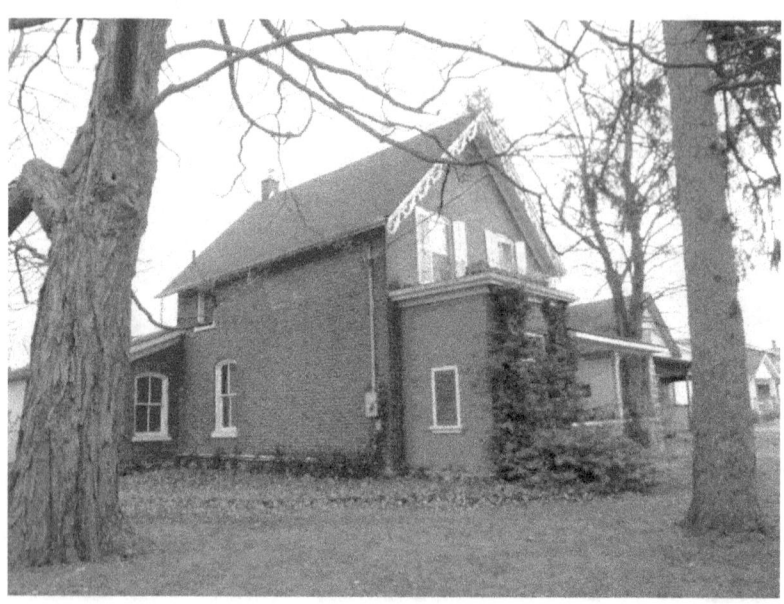

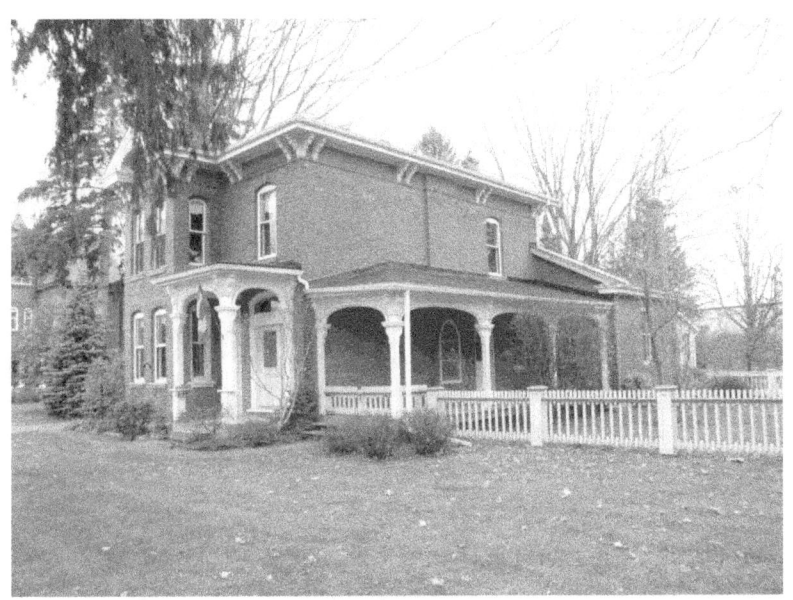

173 Main Street

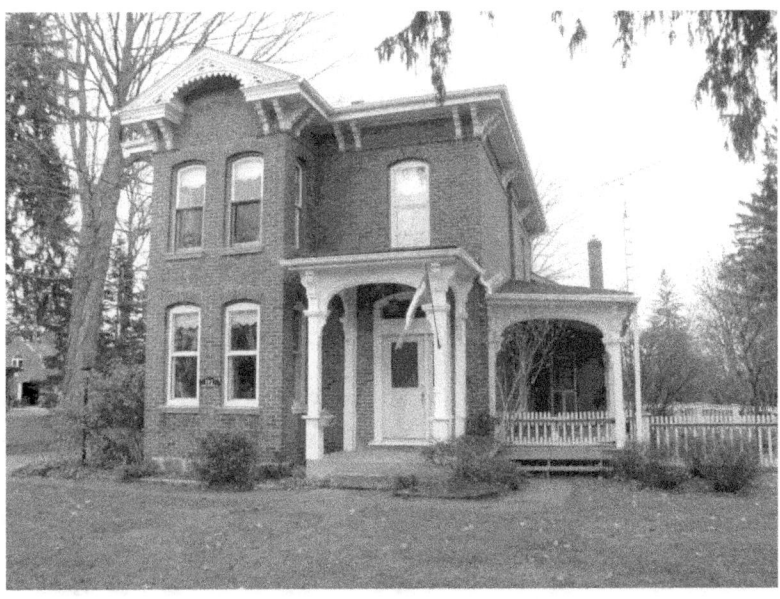

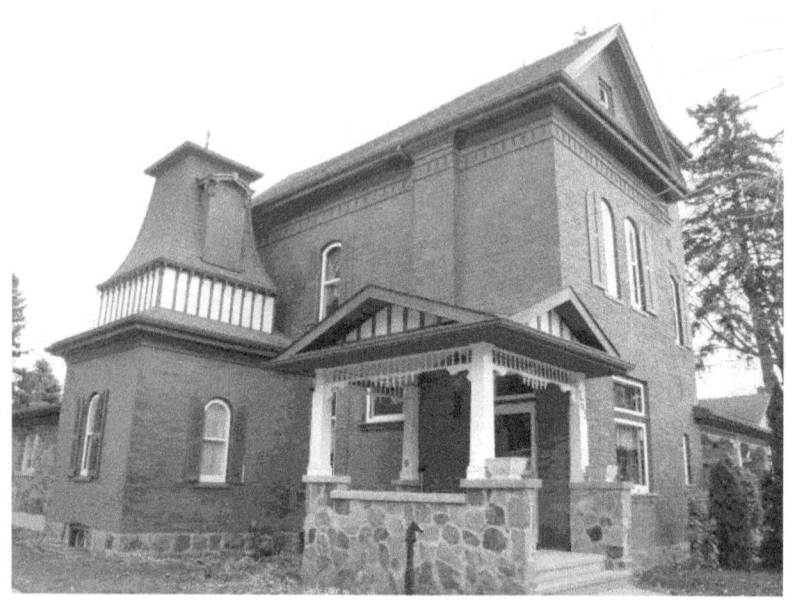

163 Main Street

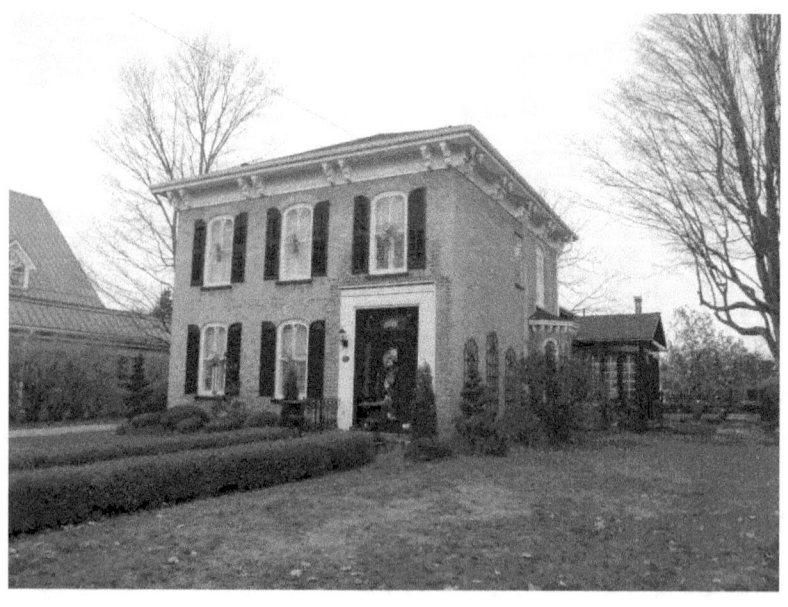

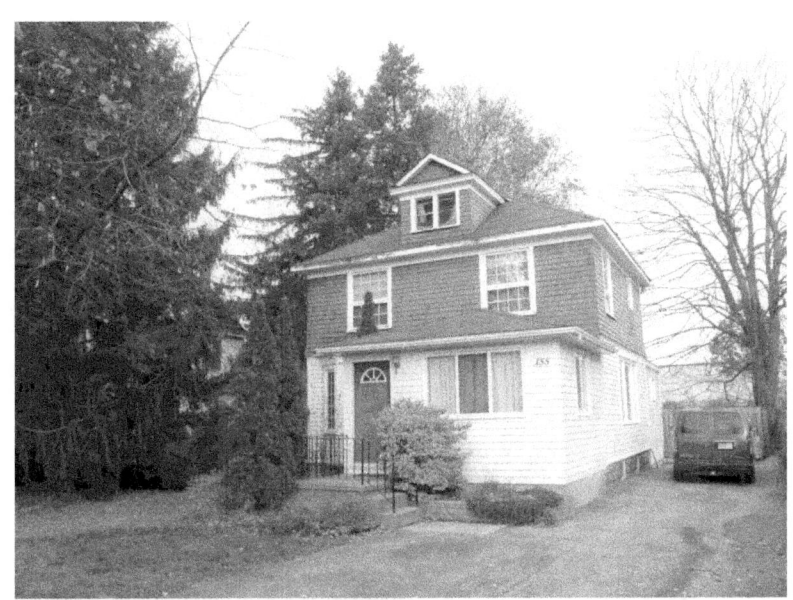

155 Main Street
Green shingled siding on upper portion of house

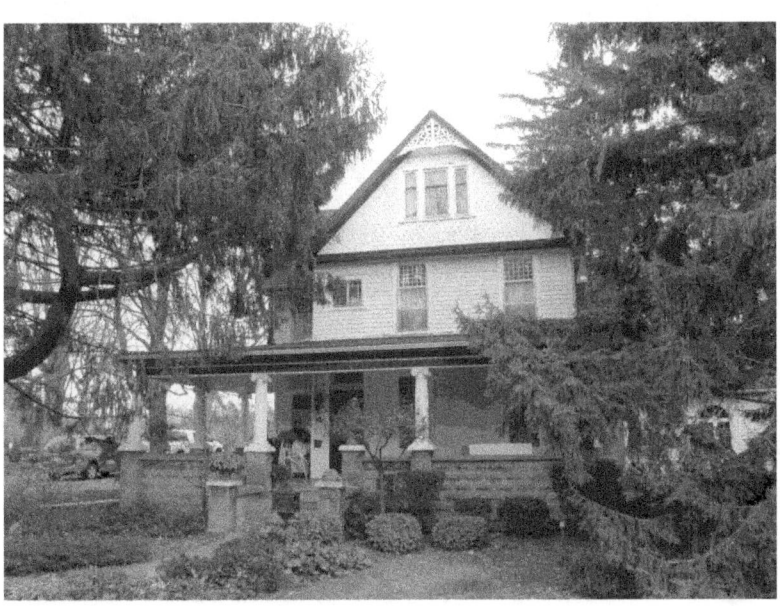

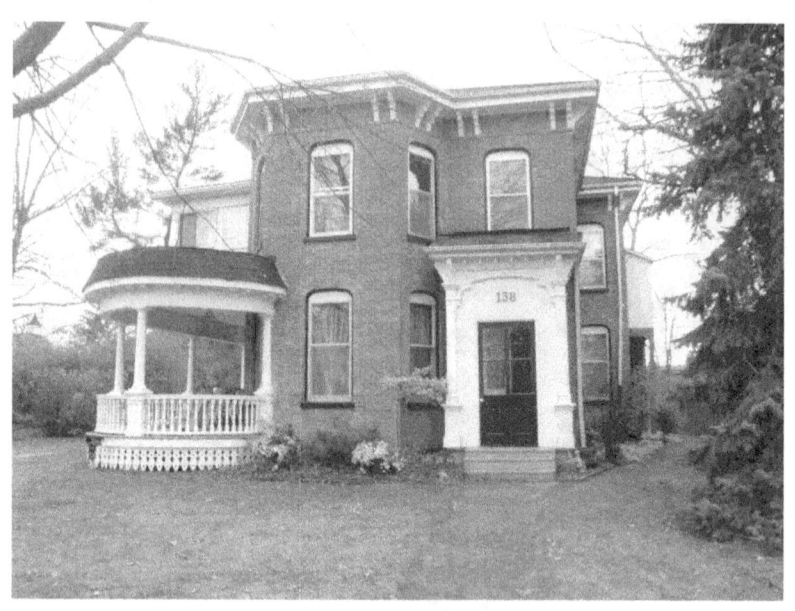

138 Main Street

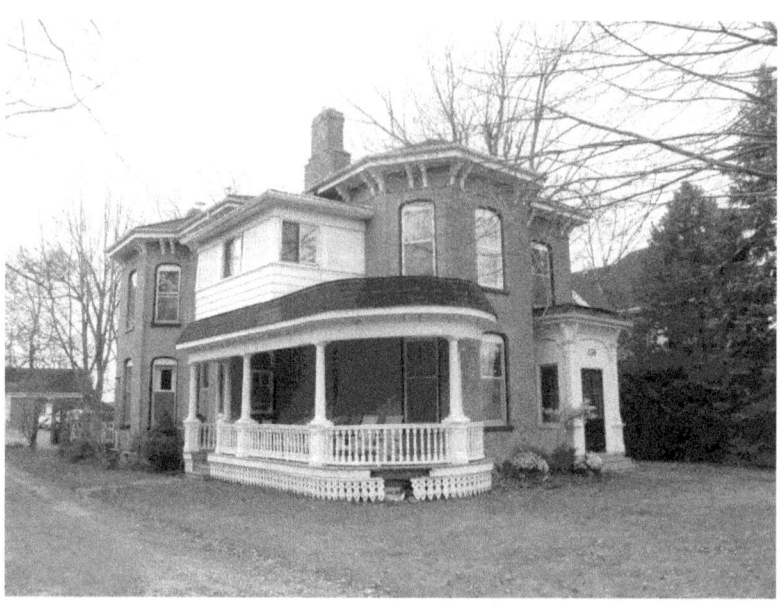

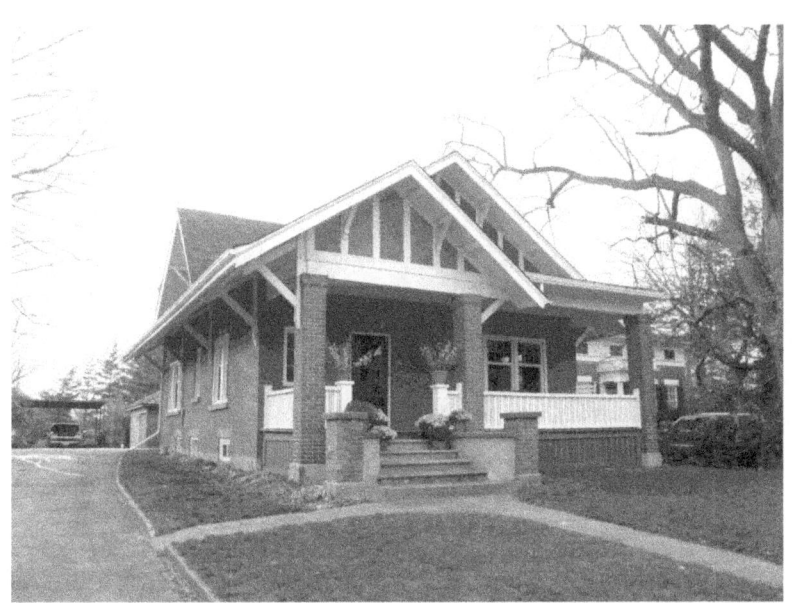

156 Main Street

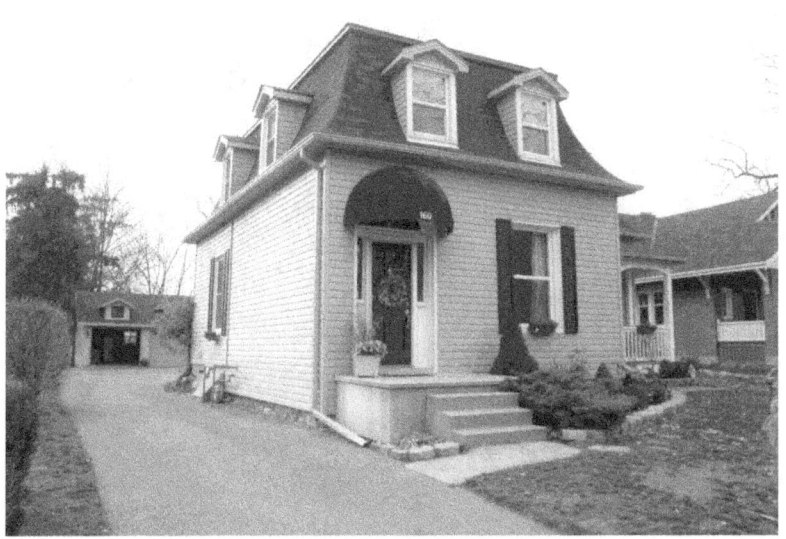

160 Main Street

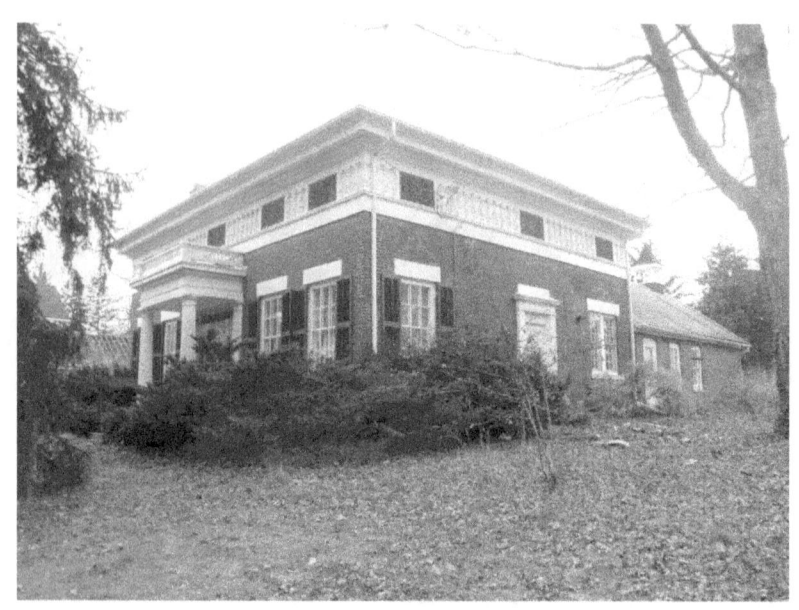

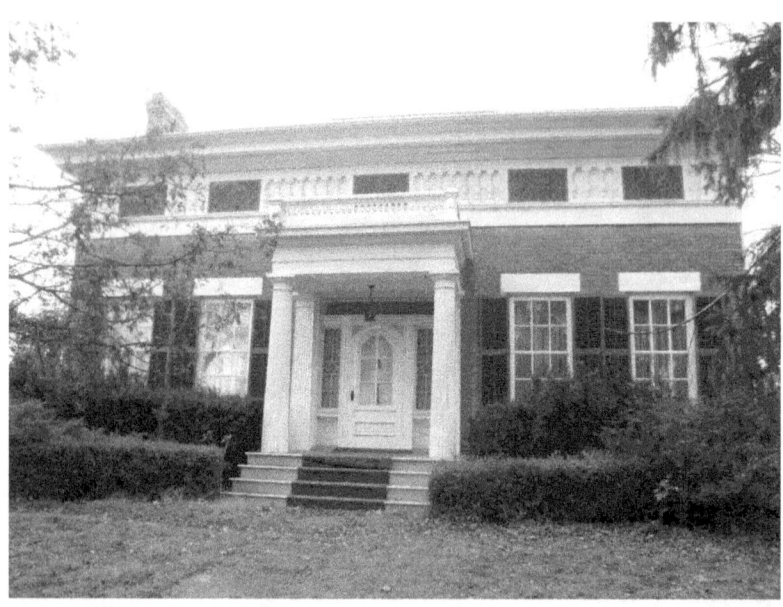

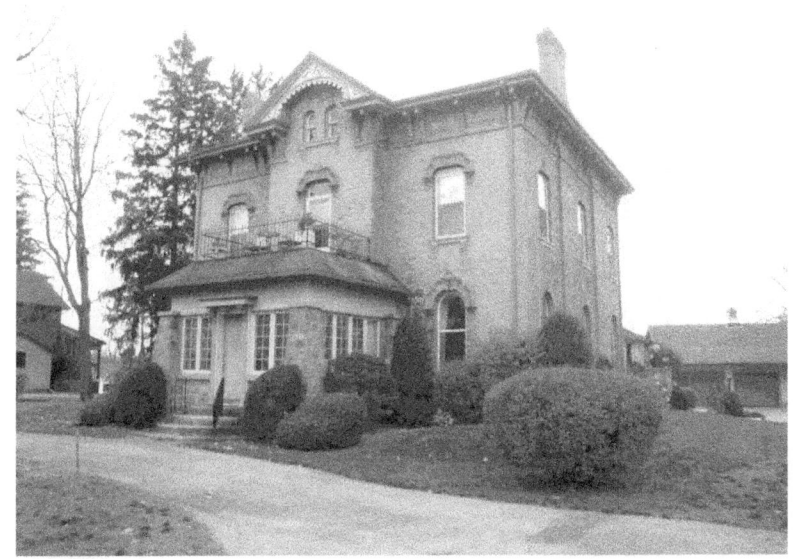

170 Main Street

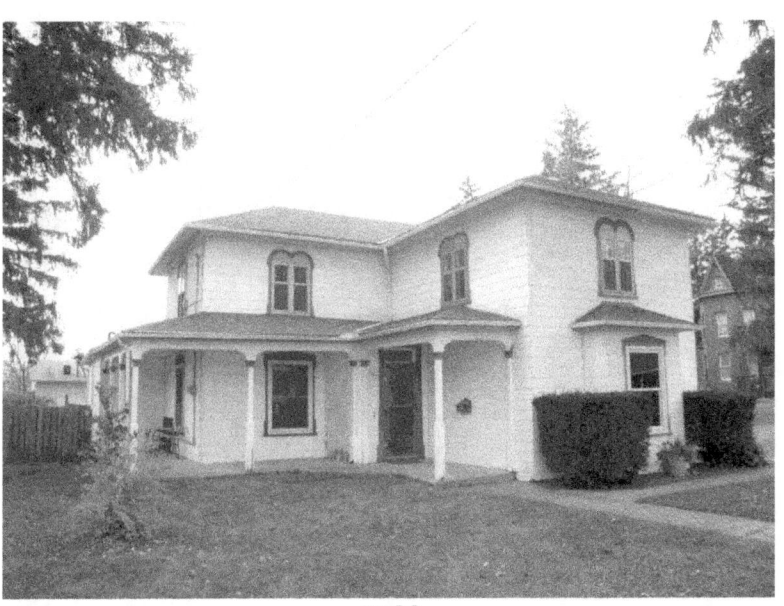

#192

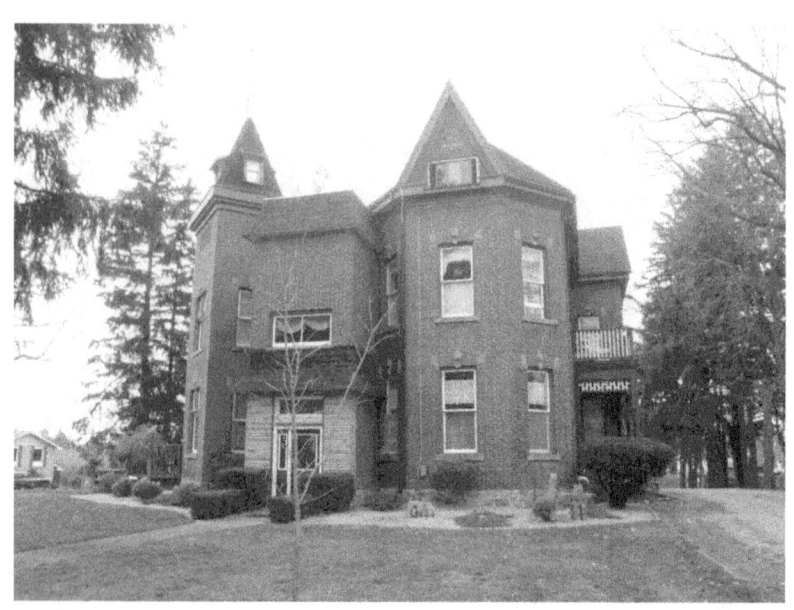

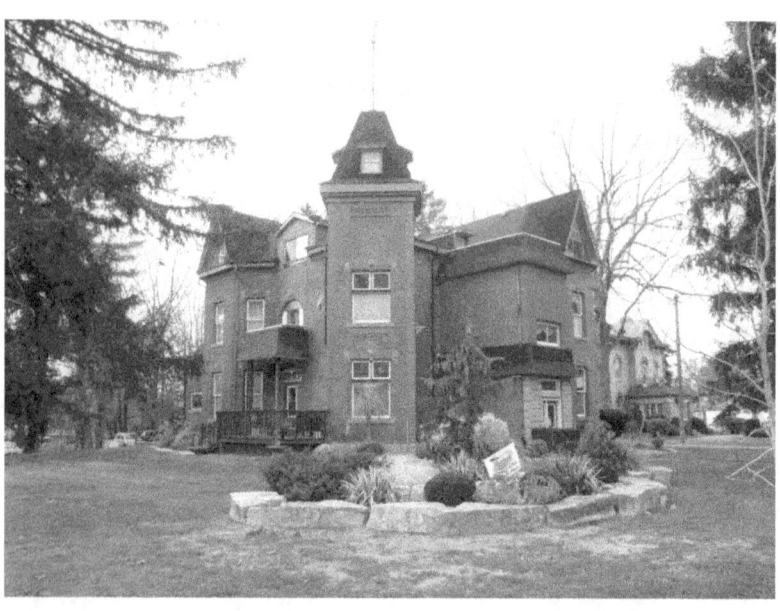

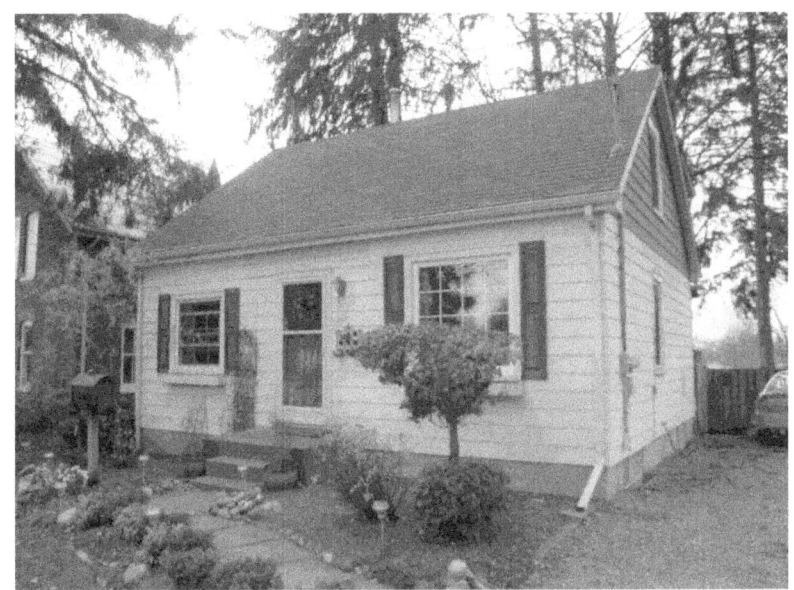

#200

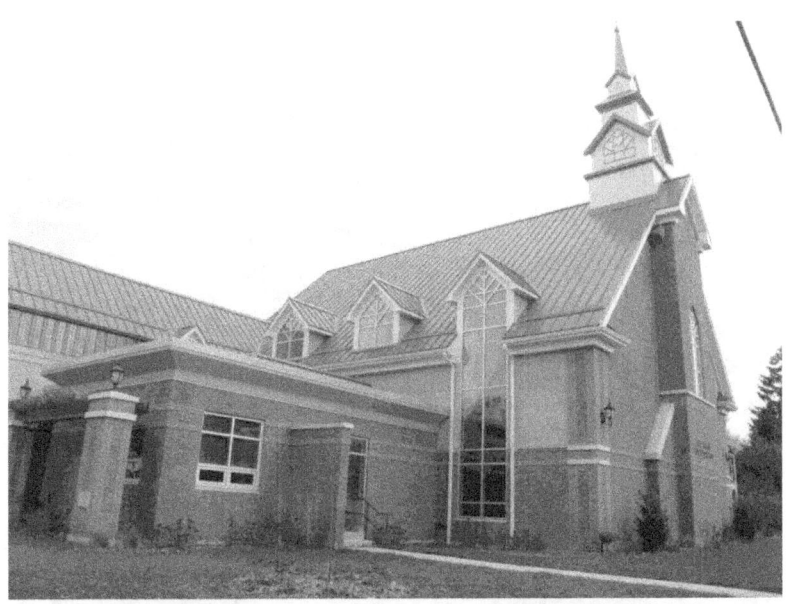

Waterford United Church rebuilt 2009-2010
135 Main Street South
(Methodist Church July 10, 1889)

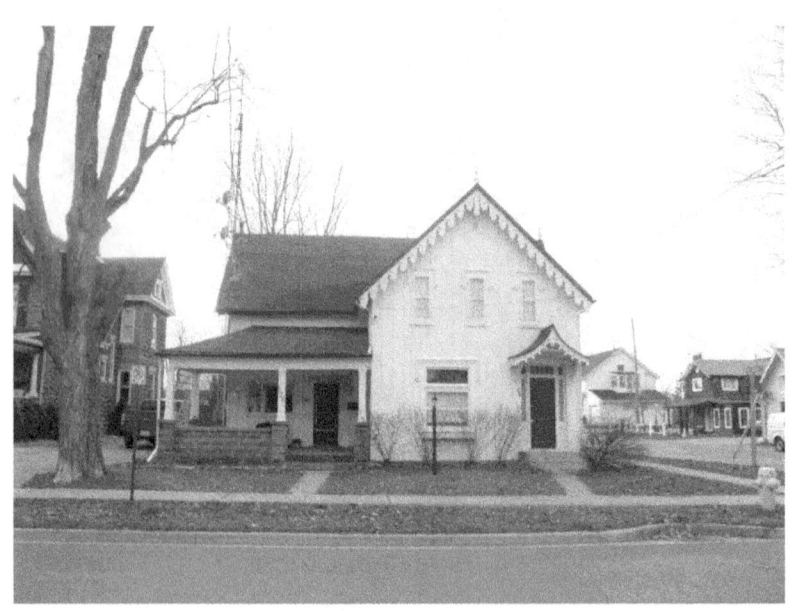

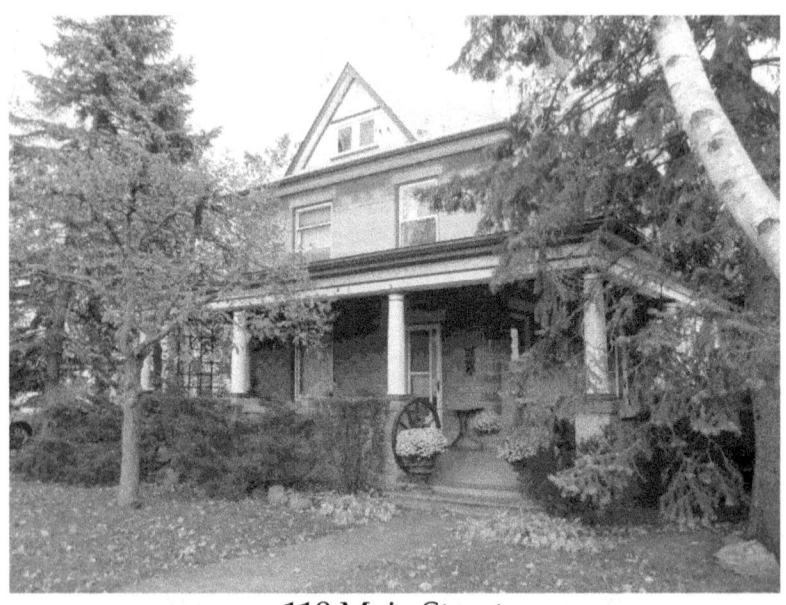

119 Main Street

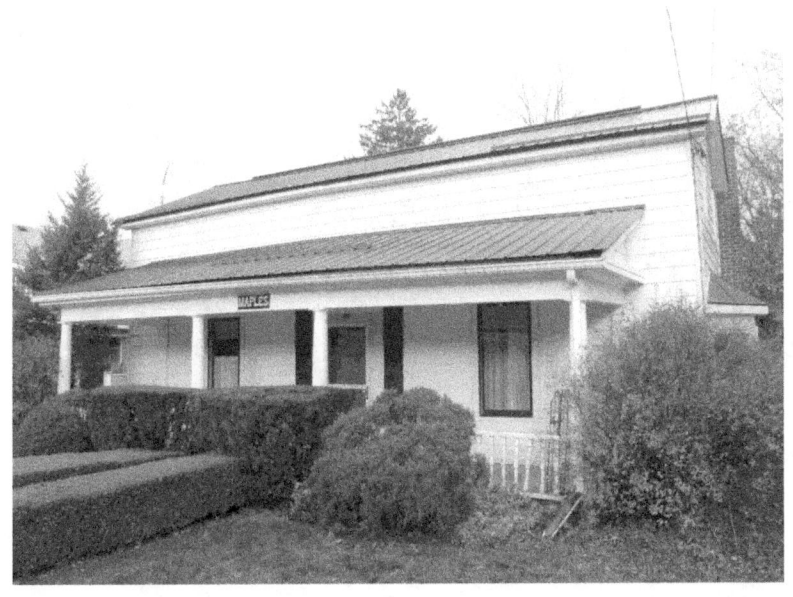

Blacksmith and Family lived here in the late 1800s
113 Main Street

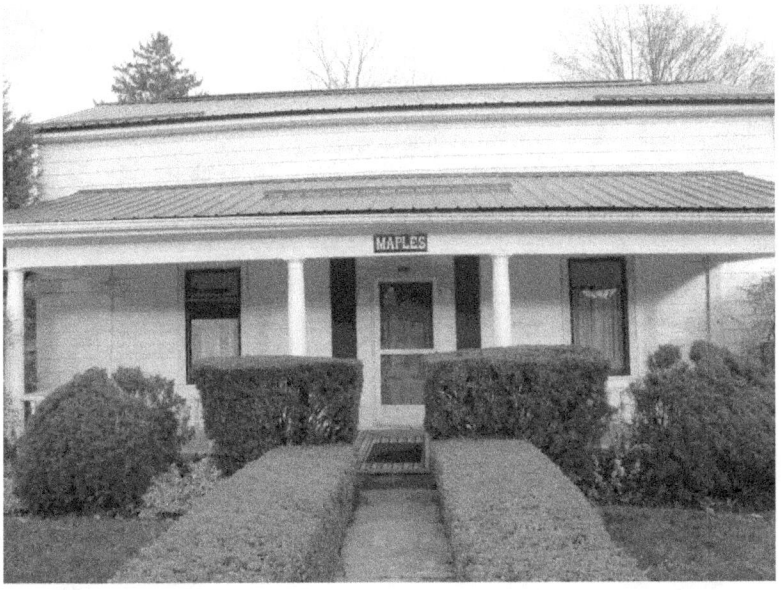

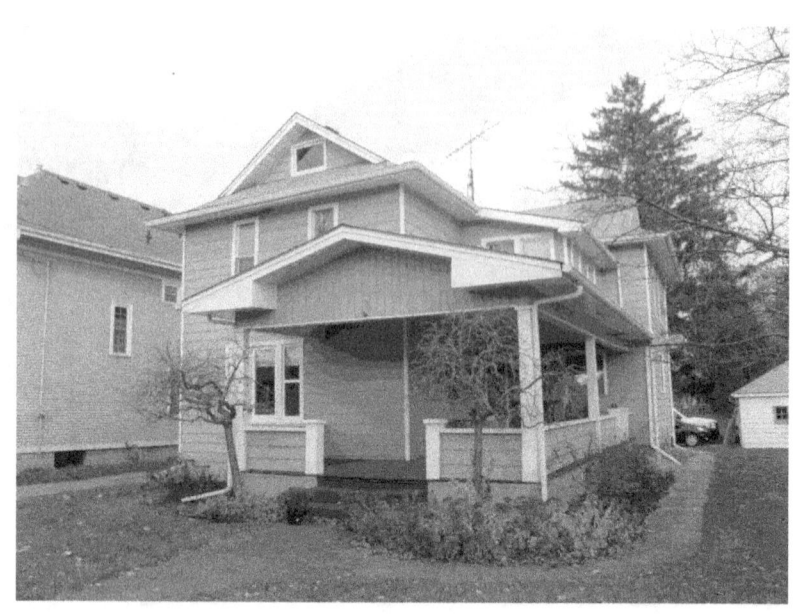

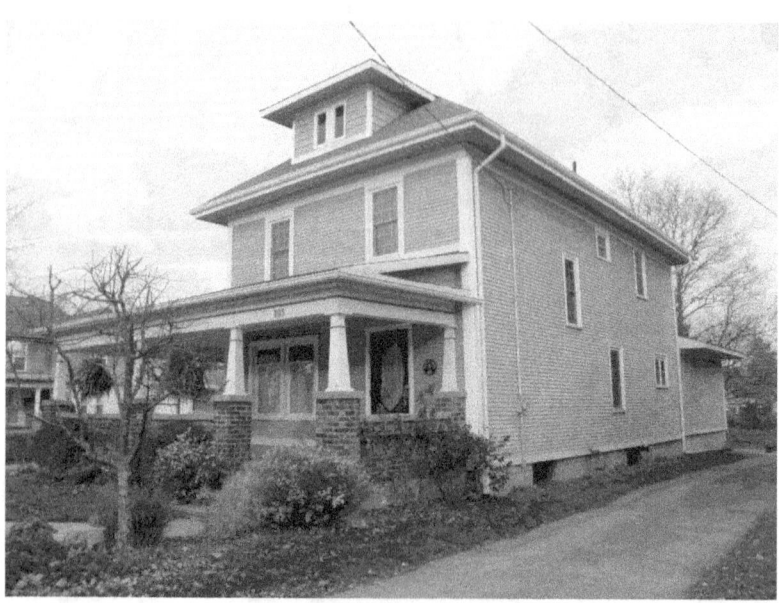

103 Main Street South

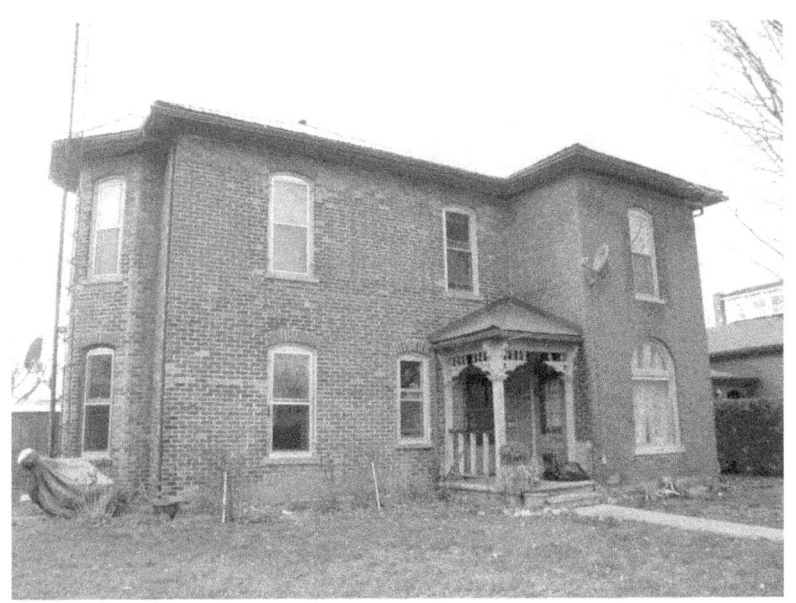

102 Main Street

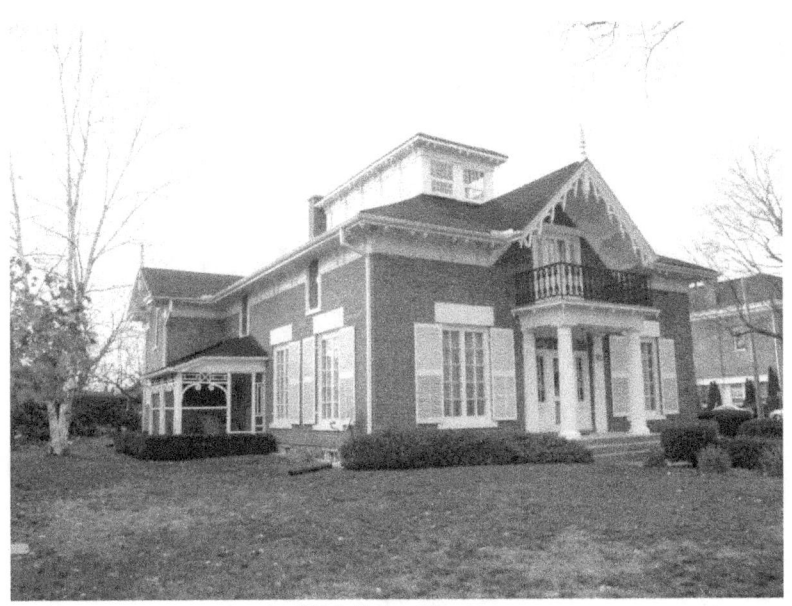

92 Main Street

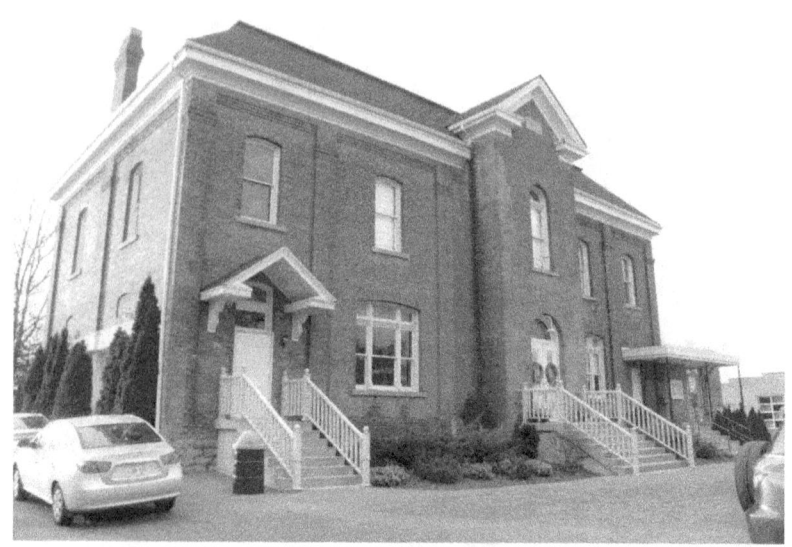

Town Hall 1902

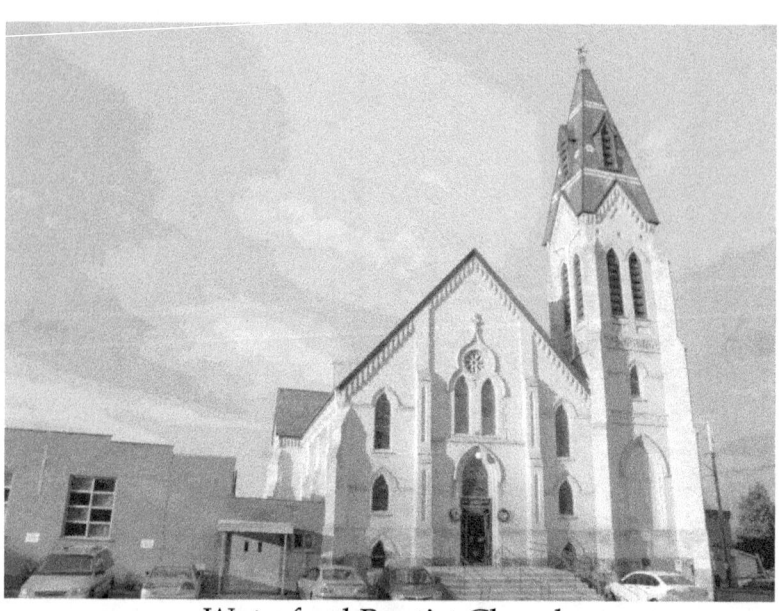

Waterford Baptist Church

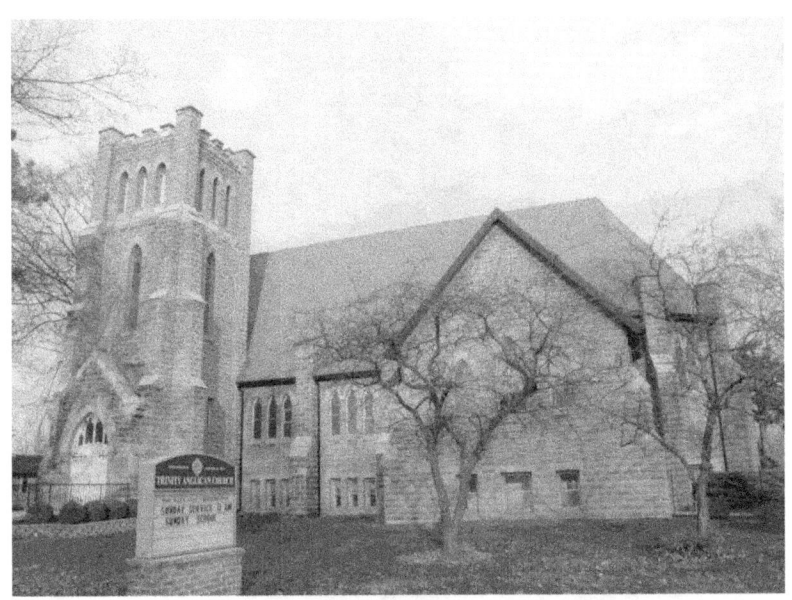

Trinity Anglican Church c. 1909
73 Main Street South

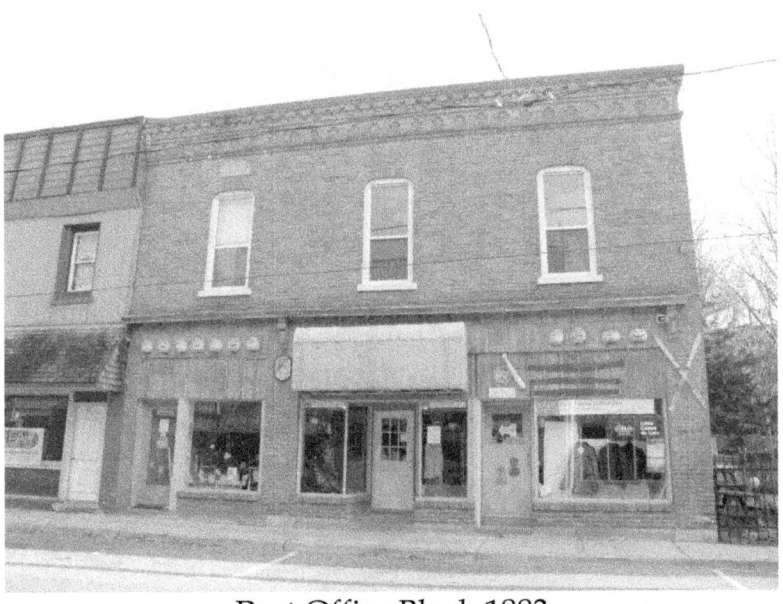

Post Office Block 1883

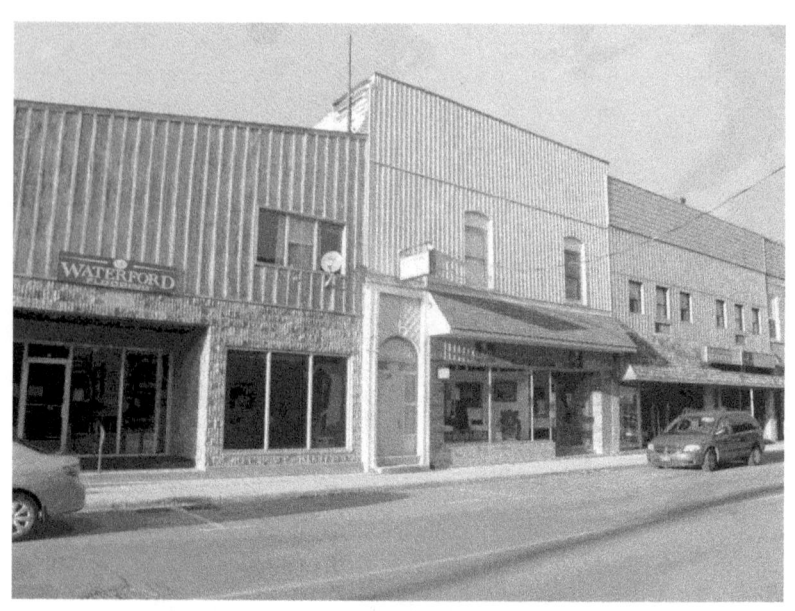

Downtown

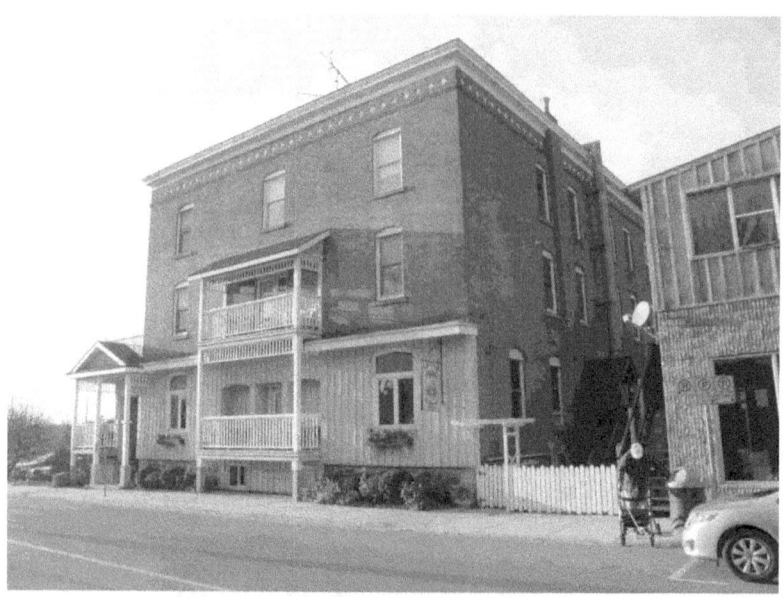

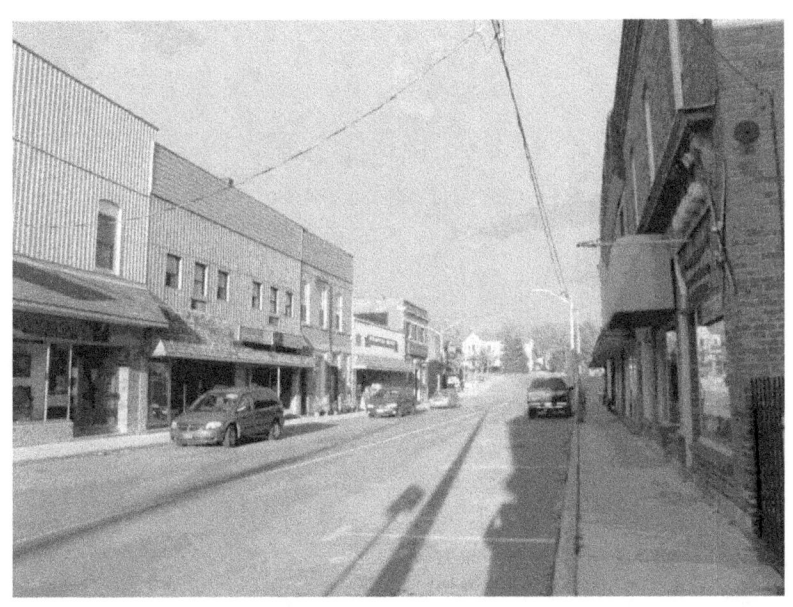

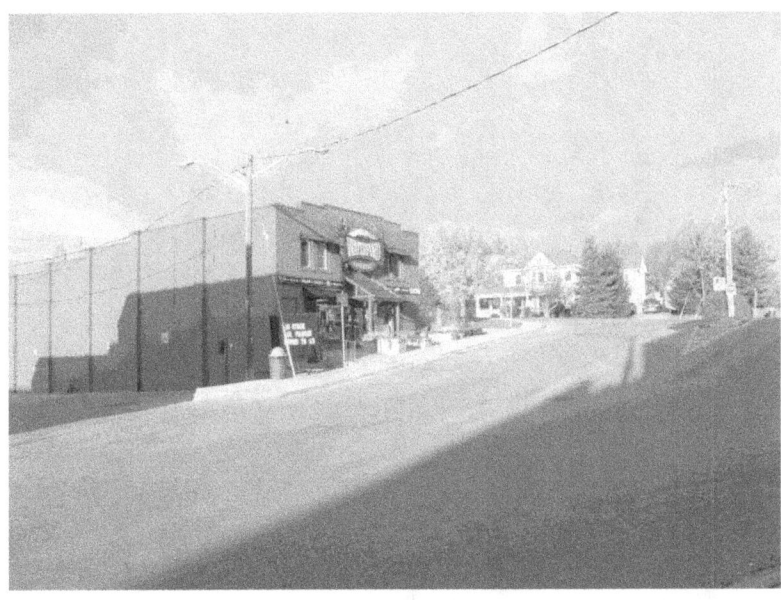

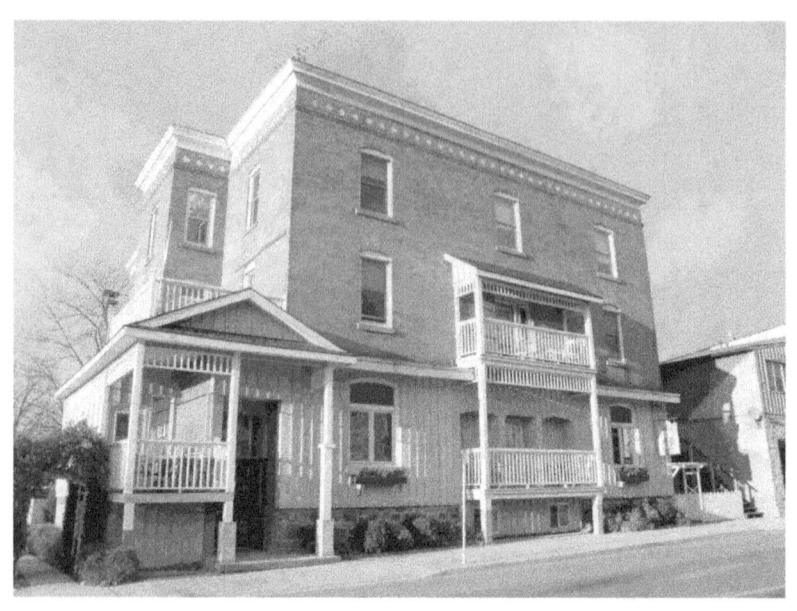

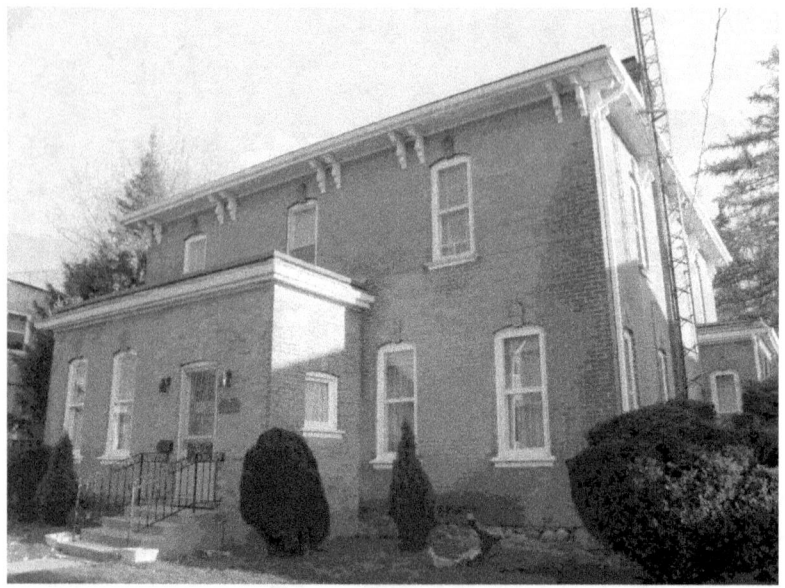

#44

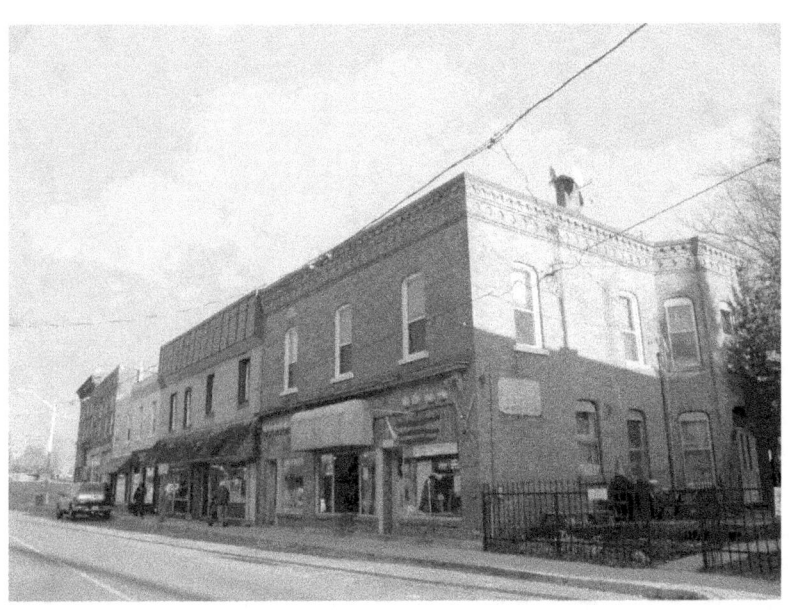

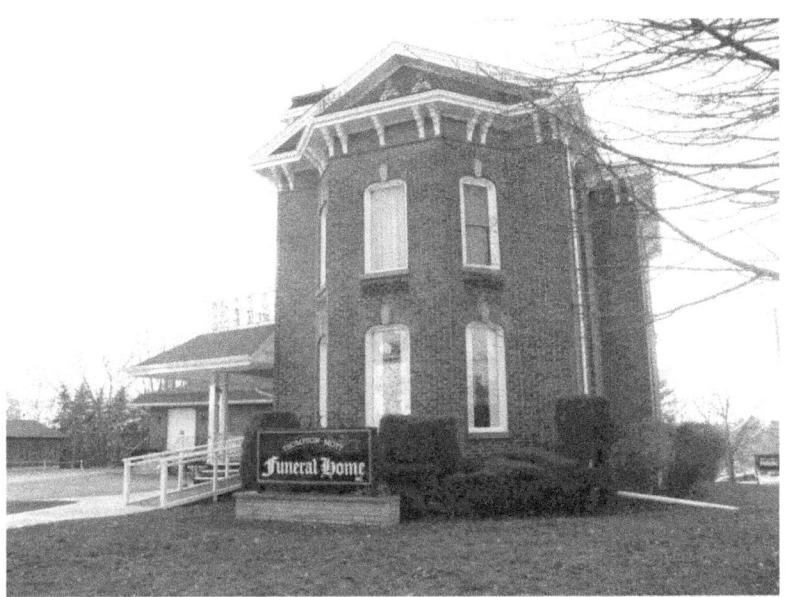

Thompson Mott Funeral Home
62 Main Street North

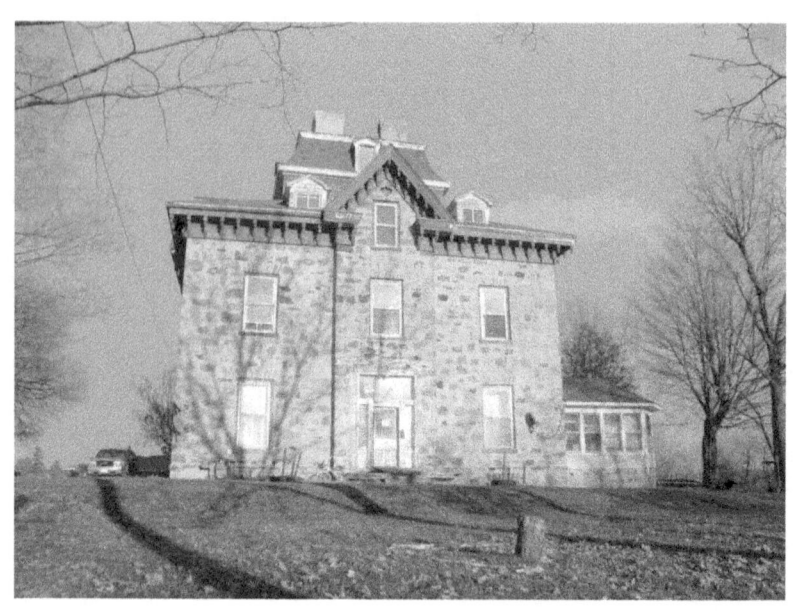

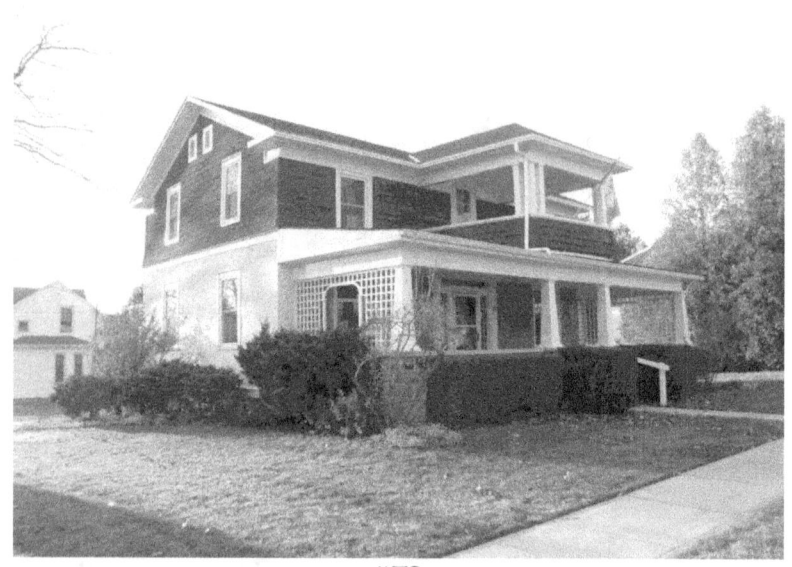

#72

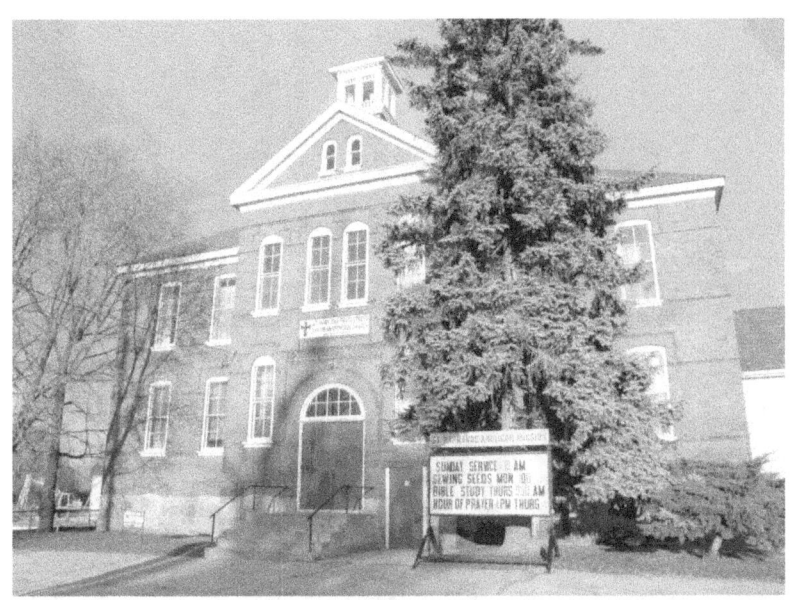

St. Mary the Protectress Ukrainian Orthodox Church
91 Bruce Street

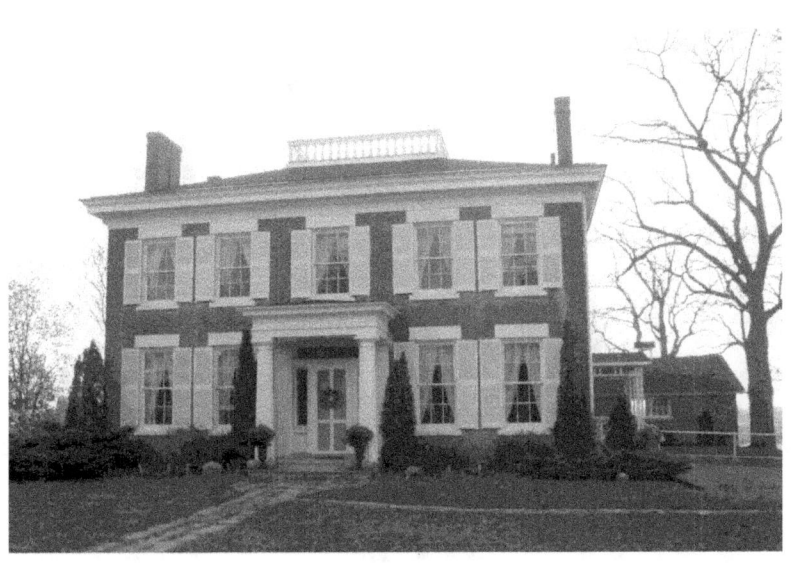

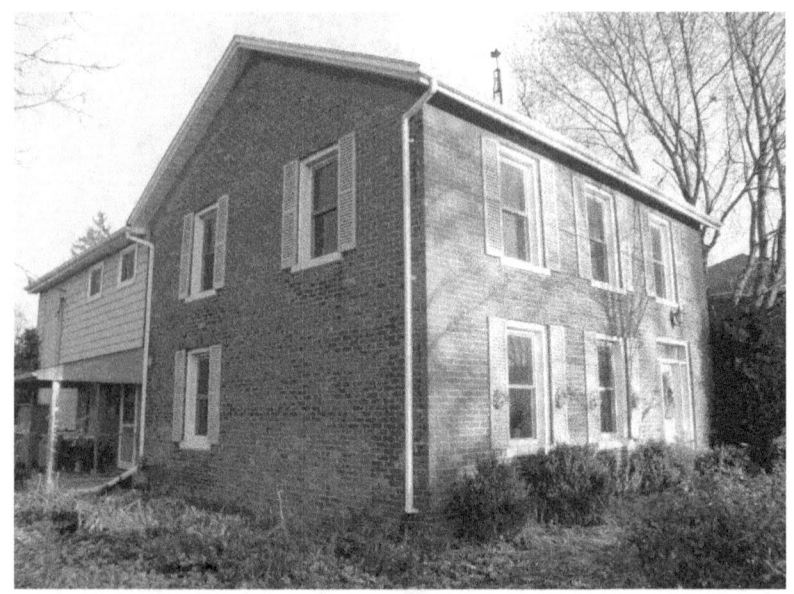

#101

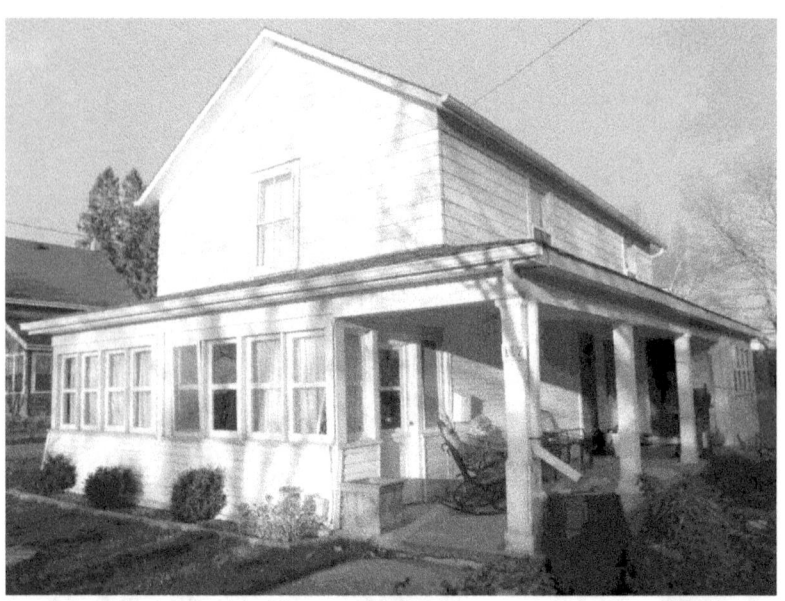

#117

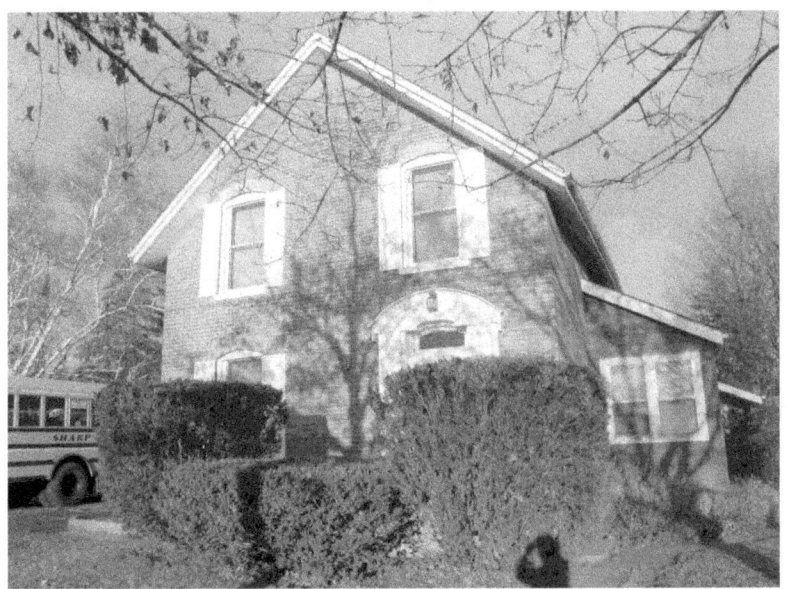

#121

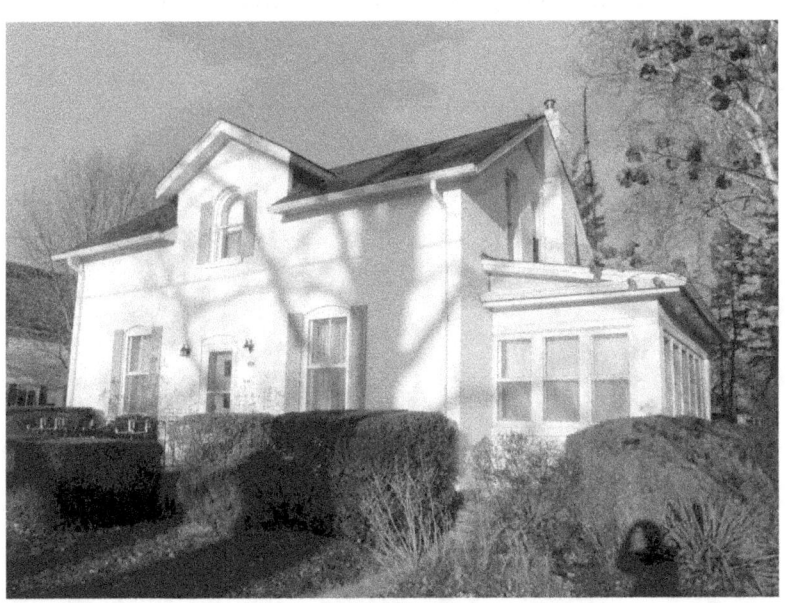

#127

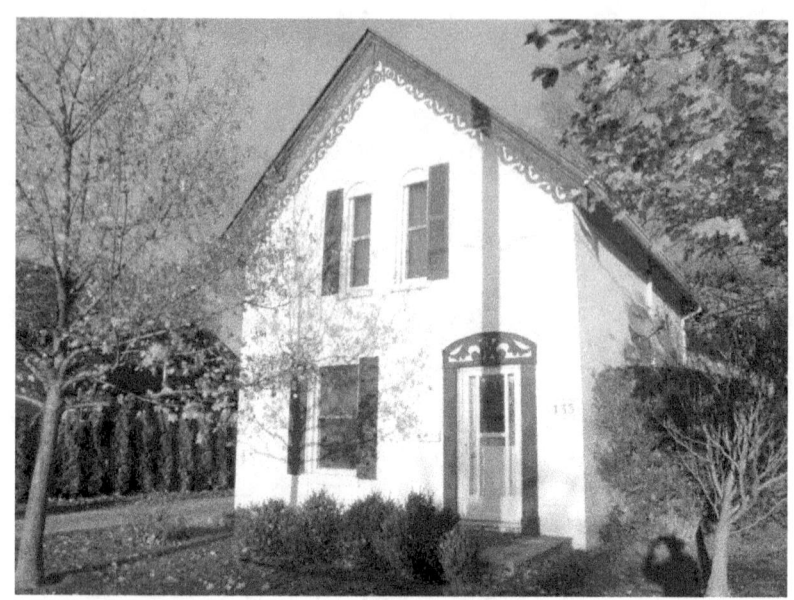

#133

Stan Pajor, Dundurn, Ontario Farm

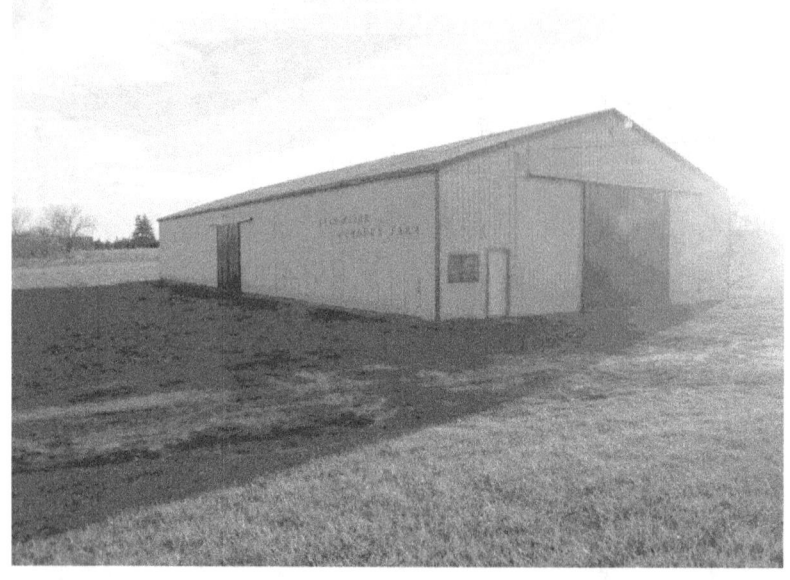

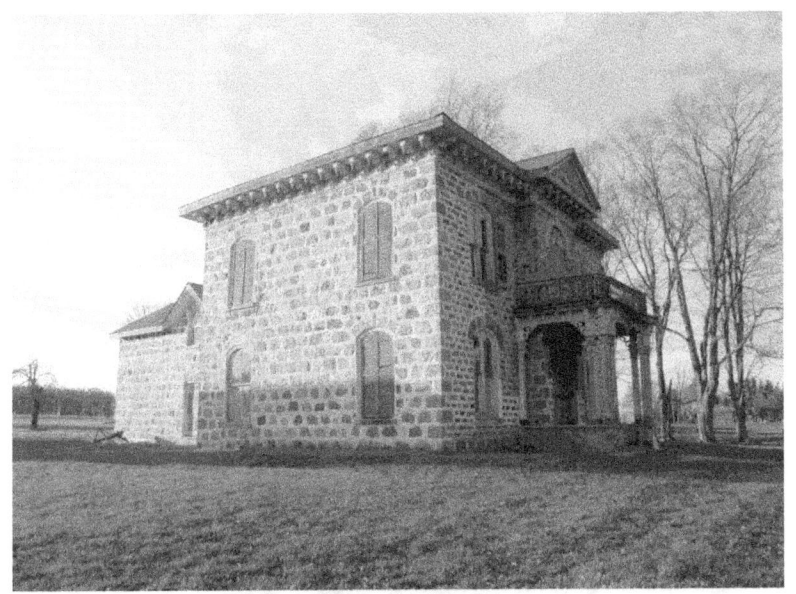

Stan Pajor Farm house

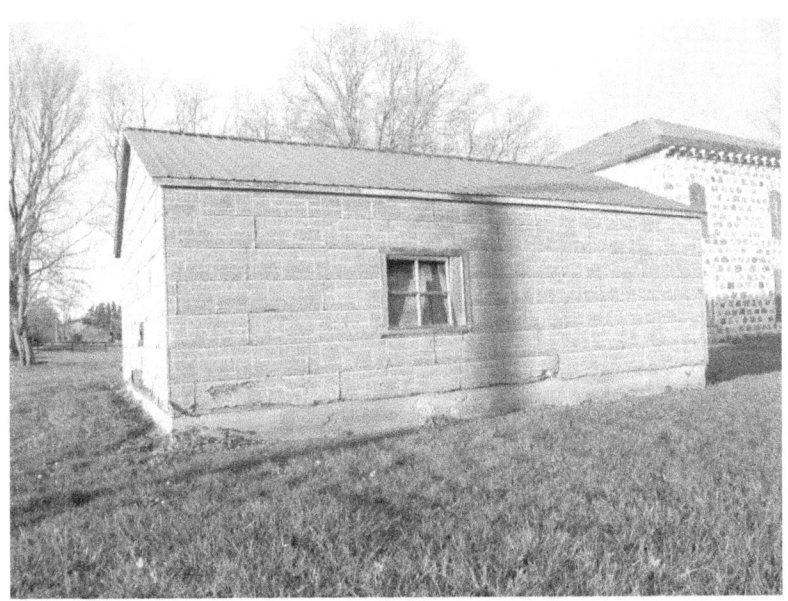

shed

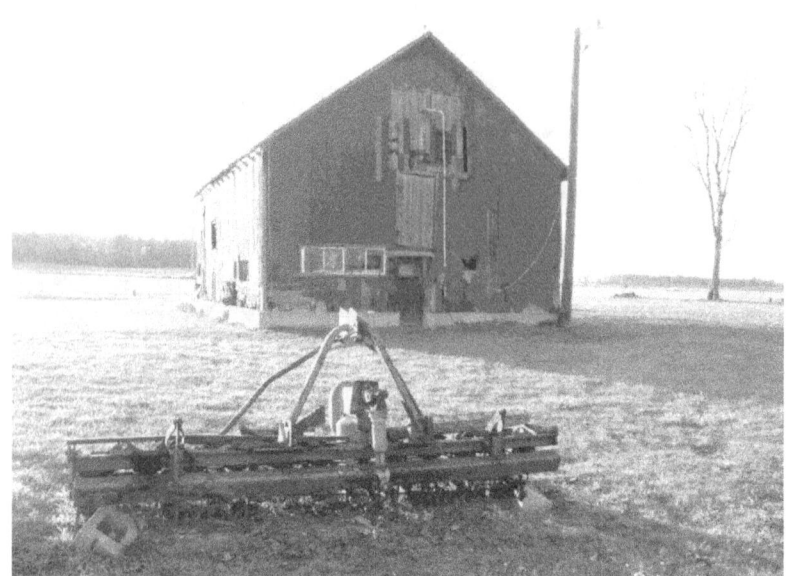

Barn

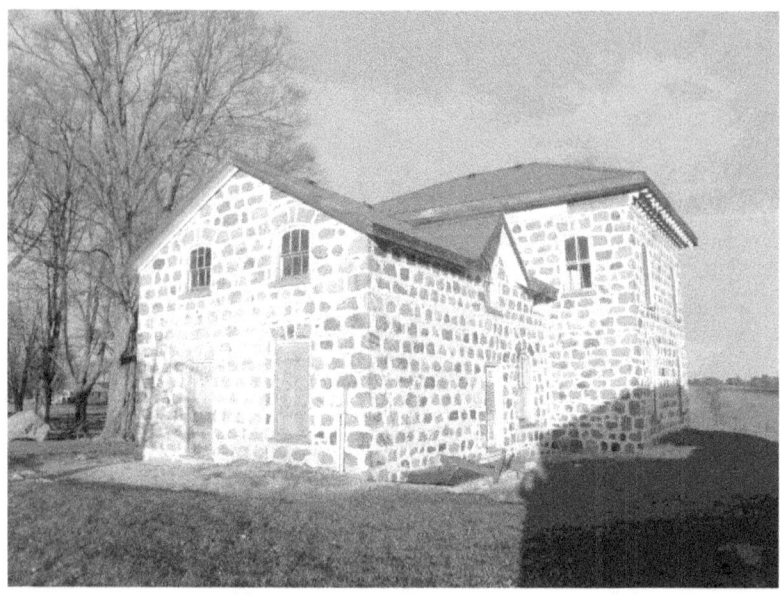

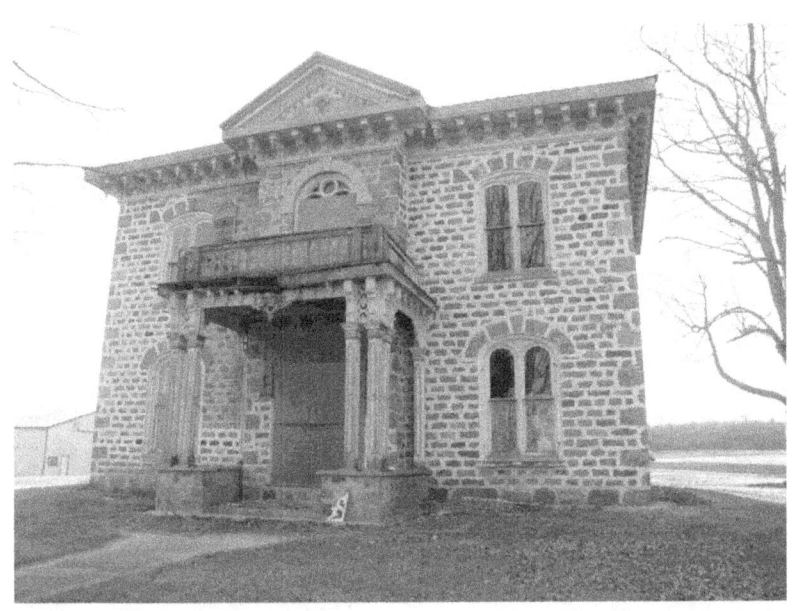

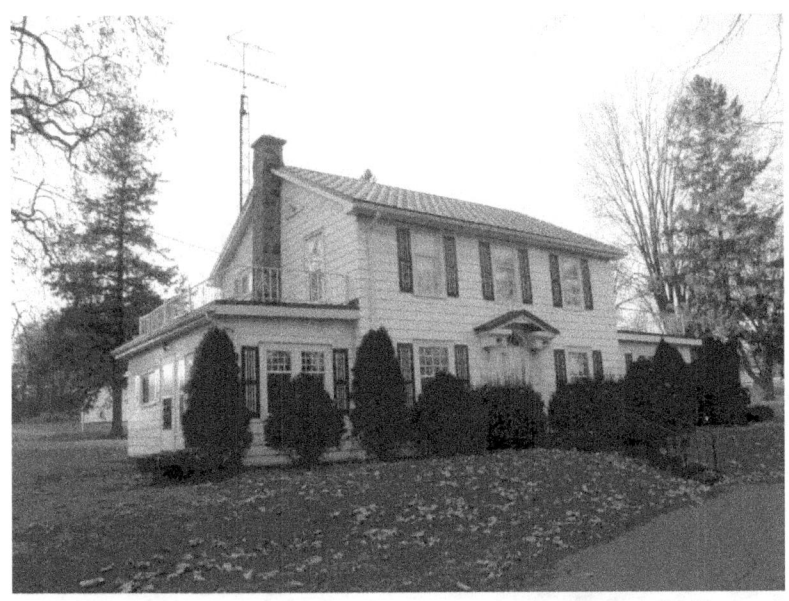

Oakland

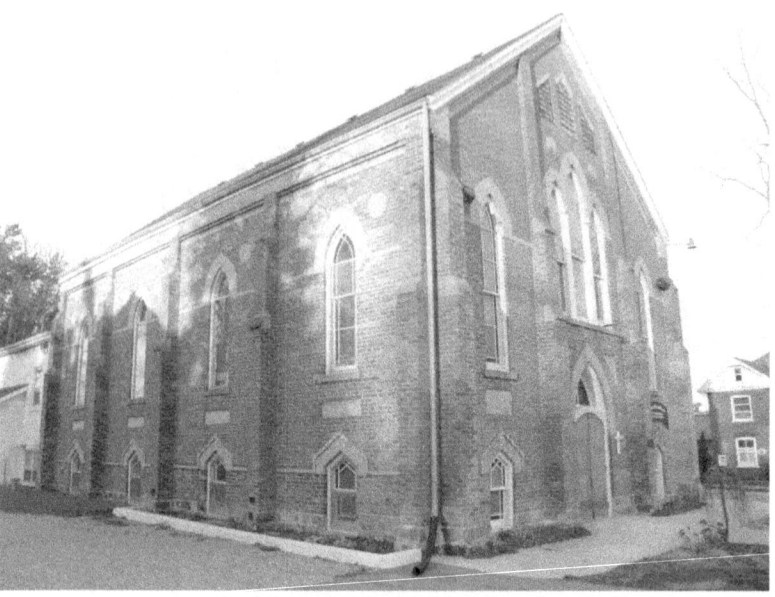

Oakland United Church
(Former Methodist Church 1886)
154 Oakland Street

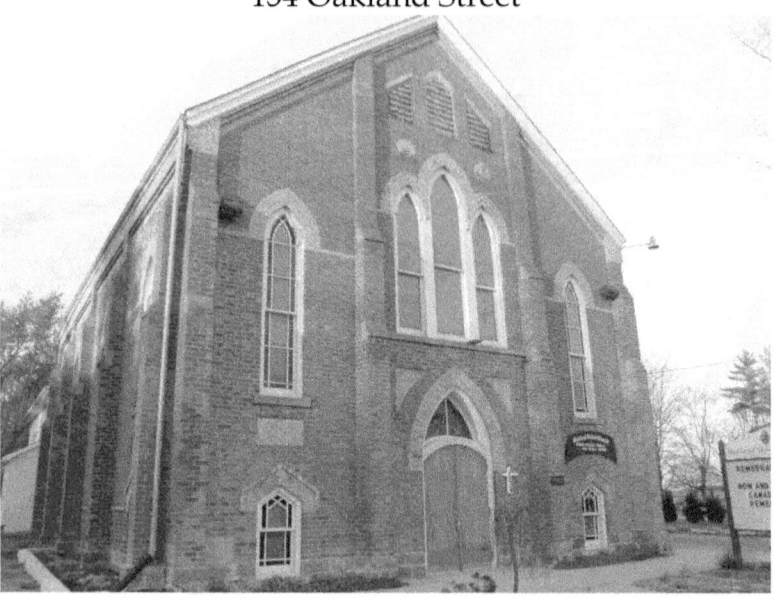

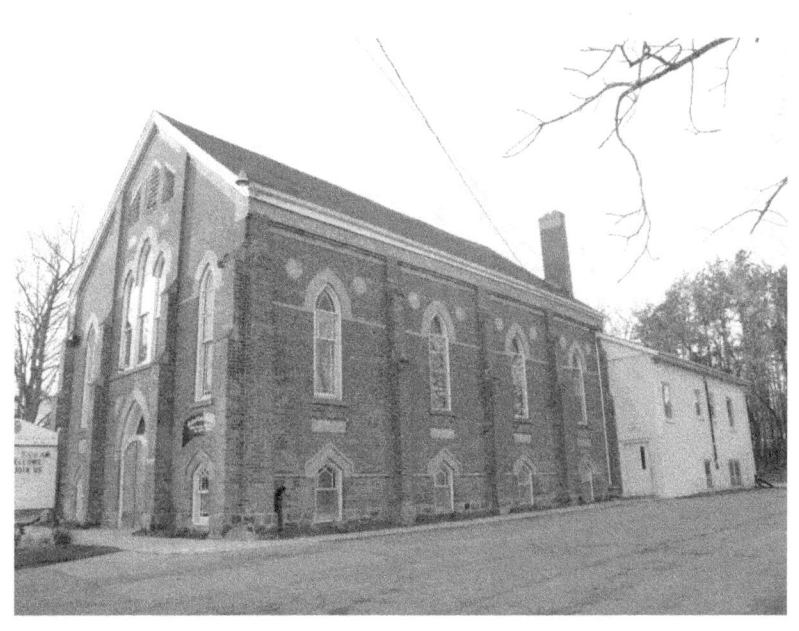

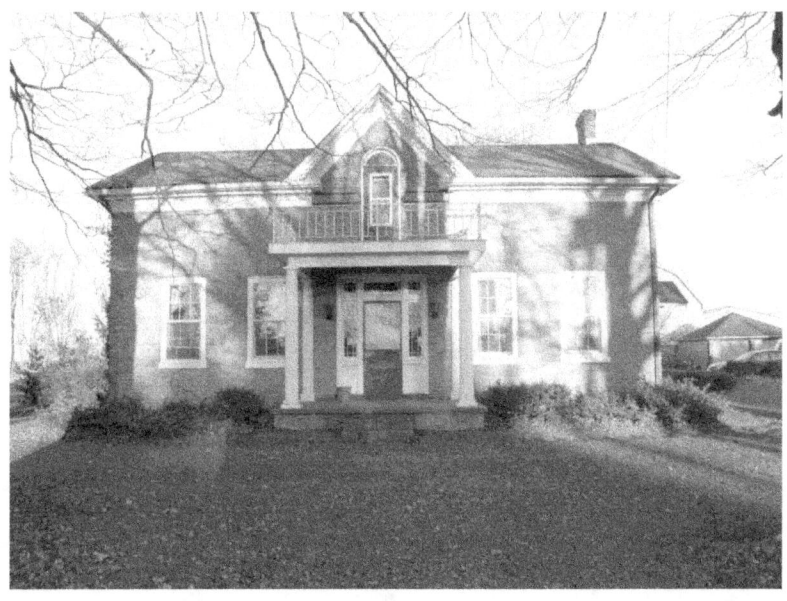

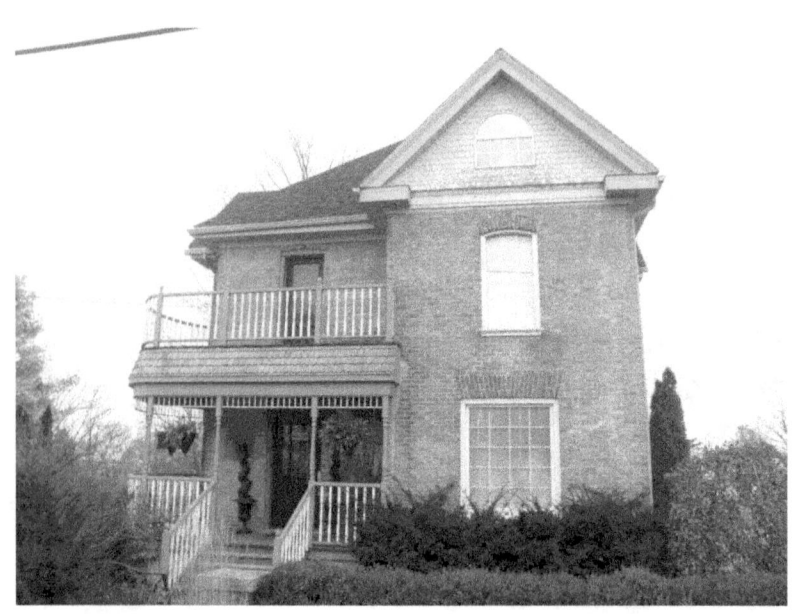

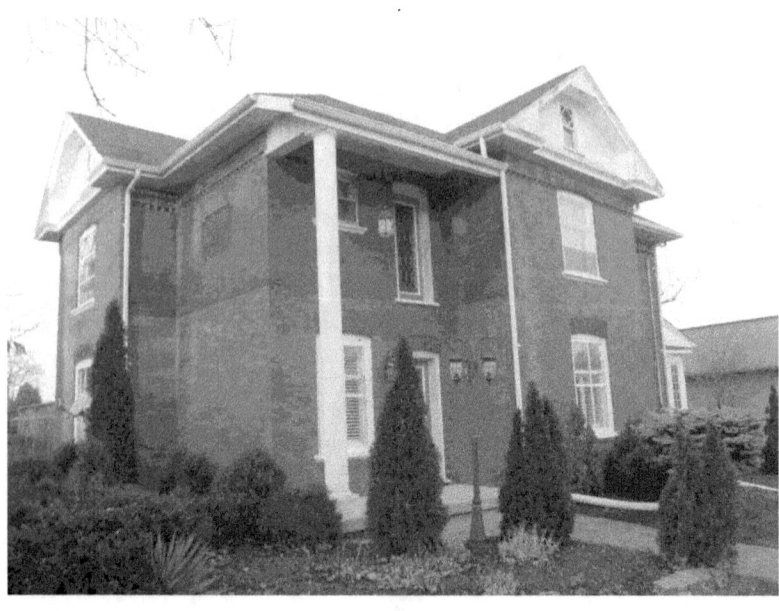

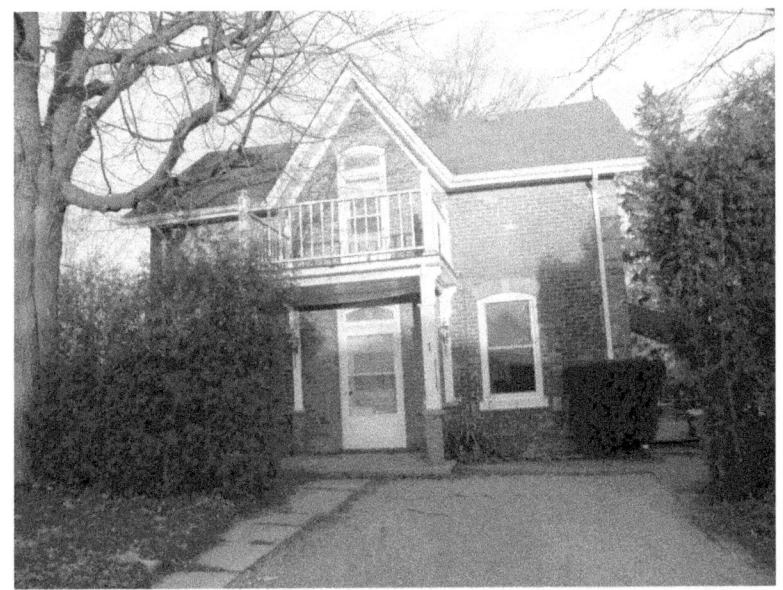

#1

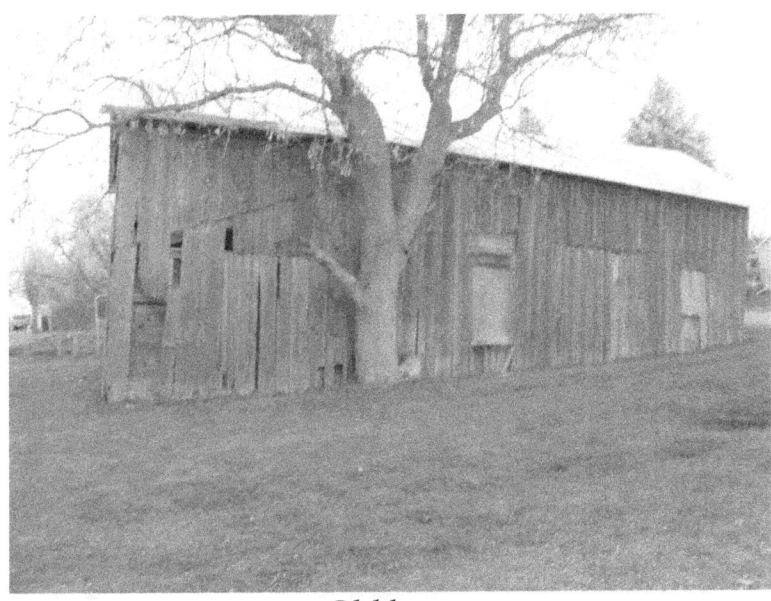

Old barn

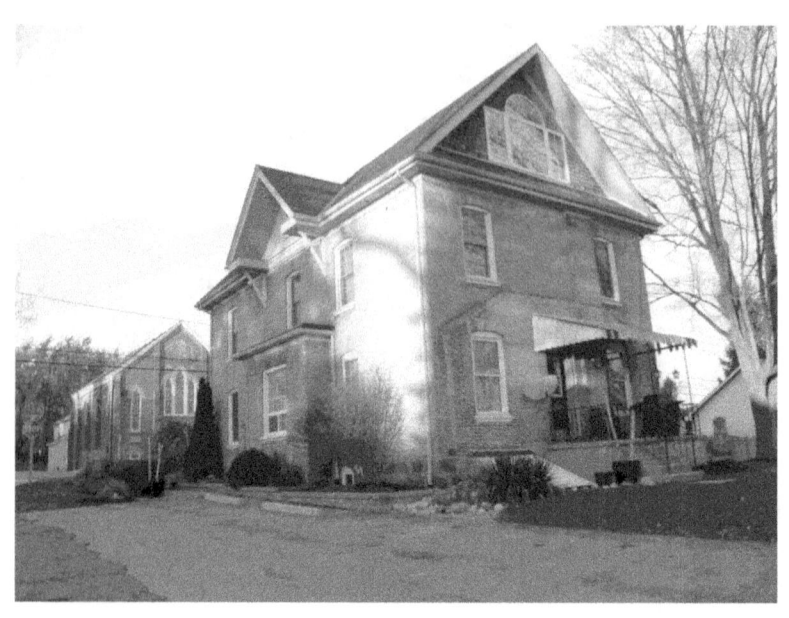

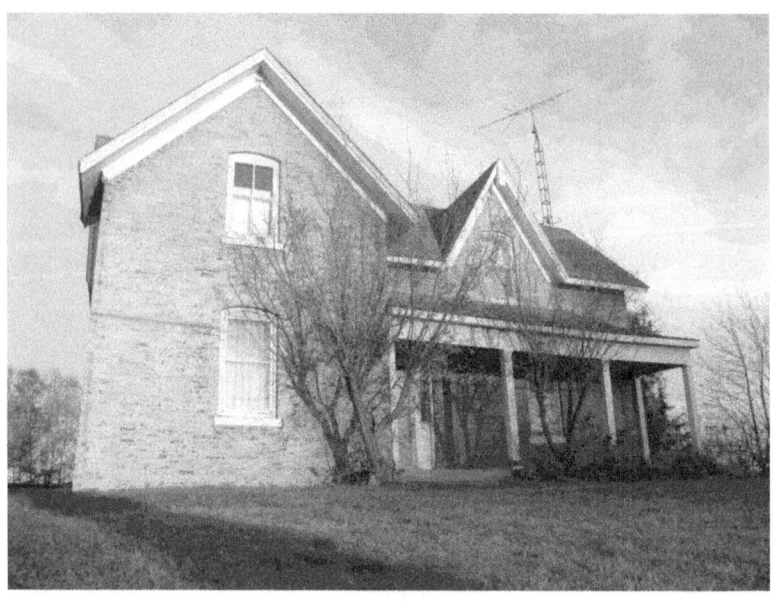